the Privilege of parenting

how to raise **great kids** in the 21st century

JAMES B. LEVINE, Ph.D.

Unwindology Publishing
Honolulu, Hawaii

The Privilege of Parenting: How to Raise Great Kids in the 21st Century
© 2003 by James B. LeVine, Ph.D.

All rights reserved. No part of this book may be reproduced or transmitted
in any form or by any means, electronic or mechanical, including photo-
copying, recording or by any information storage and retrieval system,
without express written permission from the author, except for the
inclusion of brief quotations in critical articles or a review.

Unwindology Publishing
Post Office Box 61009
Honolulu, HI 96822 U.S.A.
Orders: Unwindology@hawaii.rr.com

Printed in the United States of America
Editing by Sonia Nordenson
Book design by Sara Patton

Publisher's Cataloging-in-Publication
(*provided by Quality Books, Inc.*)

LeVine, Ph.D., James B.
    The privilege of parenting : how to raise great kids in
the 21st century / James B. LeVine.
    p. cm.
    Includes bibliographical references and index.
    LCCN 2002092134
    ISBN 0-9678106-4-7

    1. Parenting. 2. Child rearing.   I. Title.

HQ755.8.L48 2003   649'.1
                                        QBI02-200419

Contents

Introduction **1**

    Parenting Is Now Mainly Done by Substitutes 2

    The Trend to Smaller Families and Single Parenthood .. 3

    Smaller Isn't Necessarily Better 3

    Good Parenting Can Still Be Achieved 3

    New Information about Children 4

    Selecting Good Parental Substitutes Is Crucial 4

    Why Today's Parents Need to Learn More about
        Parenting 5

    Extended Families Are No More 6

    Parenting Is Life's Most Important Responsibility 7

1. Does Upbringing Matter? **9**

    What Is Upbringing? 10

    Parenting Is Mentoring 10

    Parenting Is Also Mentoring by Substitutes 11

    What Is a Child? 12

    Why Children Need Parenting 13

    Parents Are Held Accountable for How Their Kids
        Turn Out 14

    Selecting and Delegating to Parental Substitutes 15

    What This Guidebook Can Give You 17

    A Summary of Chapter One 18

    Assignment for Chapter One 18

2. The Problem with Preconceptions 20

Eliminate Faults to Avoid Passing Them Along 21

Your Children Will Assimilate Your Worldview 21

Children Are Different from Grownups 22

There Are No Surefire Methods of Influence 24

You Can't Control Children 25

It's Natural to Have Expectations for Your Children ... 26

Bring All Your Expectations Out in the Open,
Then Keep Them Under Control 26

You Needn't Teach Your Children Everything 27

Developing a Management Style 28

Children Respond to What You Do,
Not What You Say 29

You Won't Know How You've Done
Till You're Done 30

In the Meantime, How Can You Take Your
Best Guess? 30

How to Choose for Your Children 33

A Summary of Chapter Two 37

Assignment for Chapter Two 38

3. The Value of Play 39

Play Is Your Child's Most Important Function 39

Parents Should Respect Play Far More Than
They Do 40

Institutions Have Misguided Policies about Play 41

Parents Need to Be Reminded about the
Value of Play 42

A Summary of Chapter Three 42

Assignment for Chapter Three 44

CONTENTS

4. Planning for Your Children's Lives **46**

We Take Our Time Raising Our Young 47

Why Reinvent the Wheel? 47

If Extensive Parenting Is Common Sense,
Why Do Some Parents Fall Short? 48

Some Saving Graces 52

Home Base 54

Development Differences 56

Development Is Expensive, But No One Can
Afford to Go Without It 59

The Characteristics of Good Parenting 59

What Kind of Parenting Makes Children
Most Comfortable? 61

A Few Time-Proven Parenting Policies 62

What Should a Parent Do to Facilitate
Development? 75

Managing the Selection Process 77

Implementing Choices 79

Delegation Strategies 84

Othering 87

Lessons We Can Draw from the Mapping
Technique 89

A Word about Too Much Delegation 92

Listening to Your Children 94

Be Supportive, Empowering, Aware, and Positive 101

Your Values and Agenda 108

A Summary of Chapter Four 109

Assignment for Chapter Four 110

THE PRIVILEGE OF PARENTING

5. Arming Yourself First:
Your Attitudes and Strategy 111

People Are More Different Than They Are the Same . 111

Big Picture Considerations 121

Good Traits and Missing Traits................................... 123

Habits Good and Bad.. 126

Needed Skills and Not-So-Needed Skills 127

Tweaking the Mississippi 129

Seek and Connect 131

Paper and Pencil before Bow and Arrow 134

Work the Net before You Network 135

Dig Here, Dig There, But Don't Dig Everywhere 135

Survey the Forest First, Then the Trees 136

Search, Narrow, Select, Connect, Evaluate 139

Circle It, Don't Marry It 142

How to Work a Children's Fair 142

You Must Have an Attitude 148

Unfortunately, You Can't Be Fired. 150

There's No There, There—Or, Where Are the
  Emperor's Clothes? 151

A Summary of Chapter Five....................................... 153

Assignment for Chapter Five 154

6. Preparing for Takeoff 155

Maybe You're Still Not Sure 155

Programs, Programs, Programs 156

Be a Balancing Artist... 159

A Summary of Chapter Six 161

Assignment for Chapter Six 161

vi

CONTENTS

7. Now Zero In **163**
    Involve Your Children 163
    Ultimately, It's Their Decision 164
    What Will a Good Closure Look Like? 164
    What Will a Good Closure Feel Like? 165
    What If the Whole Process Fails? 166
    A Summary of Chapter Seven 166
    Assignment for Chapter Seven 167

Appendix 1.   Helpful Guides **168**
Books on:
    Toys 168
    Enrichment 168
    Play 169
    Parenting 169
    Parenting Children with Special Needs 170
    Childhood Planning 171
    Childhood Health 172
    Family Communication 173
    Single Parenting 174
    Child Development Programs 175
    Upbringing Issues 176
    Home Schooling 176
    Financial Advice 177
    Adoption 177

**Appendix 2.   Checklist of Children's Programs,
Services, and Products** **179**

Bibliography **181**
Index **184**

vii

Acknowledgments

Aside from the talented few who have helped to complete this book and have received my personal thanks, my inspiration has come from many sources, a few of which I wish to acknowledge here. First of all, I thank my parents, and additionally their parents, not only for being my faithful mentors but also for doing such a good job.

Besides incorporating my childhood experiences, this book also encompasses all the experiences I've had in the past thirty years as a parent and grandparent. These familial responsibilities brought me quite an awakening, and I have my three children and five grandchildren, as well as the two mothers of my children, to thank for that.

A further motivation behind *The Privilege of Parenting* was my participation in the operations of a yo-yo company—one in which our principal responsibility was training children in the use of these toys. Watching those young people play reconnected me with what's important in life.

This book also came into being because of many discussions I've had with Sue Parry, a mother well-read in issues of children's upbringing. Sue opened my eyes to the many problems facing children and parents today.

I am grateful to the following reviewers who have given unselfishly of their time to critically go over every line of every paragraph I set down: Dr. Audrey Skrupskelis, Professor of Early Childhood Education, University of South Carolina;

ix

THE PRIVILEGE OF PARENTING

Dr. Georgiana M. Duarte, Associate Professor of Early Childhood Education, University of Texas at Brownsville; Nancy P. Alexander, Northwestern State University Child and Family Network; Rhonda L. Clements, Associate Professor of Physical Education and Sport Services, Hofstra University; Eileen Lichtenstein, President of Balance and Power, Consultant in Meditation Fitness; Joanne Dusel, Professor of Kinesiology, Towson University; Sarah Mellow Temple, Educational Partnership Coordinator, School's Out Washington, Seattle, Washington; Dr. Tom Reed, Professor, University of South Carolina School of Education at Spartanburg; Dr. Marianne Torbert, Temple University, Philadelphia, Pennsylvania; Brian Ashley, Sociologist and Pedagogue, Editor-in-Chief, *International Play Association Journal,* Stockholm, Sweden; and Nancy Heathman, Accreditation Project Specialist, Heart of America Family Services, Kansas City, Kansas.

Finally, I've been inspired by the many authors listed in the bibliography — individuals who have concerned themselves with child rearing and have thereby enriched my mind with numerous insights.

Foreword

All who are concerned with children and their development in modern society know the importance of upholding the family as a child-fostering institution. As one who has spent a lifetime's professional career working with social problems and training professionals to help people cope with the stresses of modern society, I have seen too much of the effects of lack of nurture in childhood.

The fact that modern society is shaping new family forms, such as one-parent families, increases all parents' need for support and information in their nurturing role. Optimally, this support will retain the elements of good advice and practice that epitomized the neighborliness of the old social forms and community relations that are now disappearing. These old ways were typified by the common sense and easy communication of a local culture, now often frowned upon in a society of experts and specialists.

Parents, in their nurturing role, still need to find this kind of easily understandable message that is based upon a clear knowledge of their everyday situation. This is what Jim LeVine has provided in this excellent revision of homespun advice underpinned by an understanding of the research and expert knowledge of modern child development.

Because Jim LeVine is himself an experienced parent, and one who has not forgotten how it was to be nurtured in a stable society with a wide network of relationships, his advice is even more relevant. Parents and child care givers of today, especially the very young, have not, from their own background, the certain and secure recognition of what is best for children. Add that to the increasing complexity and the swift changes and innovations of the modern society and it is not difficult to understand the desperate thirst that parents have for some confirmation that their attempts to help their children grow into the wider world have some support. This is what they will find and recognize in Jim LeVine's readable publication.

– Brian Ashley, sociologist, editor of *PlayRights* magazine
and an officer of the International Play Association,
an advocacy group for children

Preface

A CHILD, GRANDCHILD, PARENT, AND GRANDPARENT

*The trouble with using experience as a guide is that
the final exam often comes first, and then the lesson.*

– Unknown

My primary qualification for writing this book is that I had a
glorious upbringing by two of the best parents ever, in one of
the greatest places in the world to be brought up: Hawaii.
And I think I can say that I have, in turn, successfully handed
down the parenting knowledge I gleaned from my parents to
my own children.

Another qualification is that I am now a child, a grand-
child, a parent, and a grandparent—all at the same time. This
makes me, in a certain sense, omniscient when it comes to
child rearing; I can share my diverse views without prejudice.

I'm also a student, teacher, and bon vivant, with thirty-six
years of formal education to my credit as well as fifty-seven
years of informal play. I've read thousands of books, stories,
and articles concerning children, and have written on that
and other subjects nearly every day for most of my life. I play
and laugh a lot because I want the spirit of my childhood to
remain strong in me.

Probably the most important motivating factor in writing this book comes from the implications of the following

xiii

THE PRIVILEGE OF PARENTING

horrifying statement by Dr. Lawrence Diller in his recent book, *Should I Medicate My Child?*

> *Approximately 5 million children in America take at least one psychiatric drug; the number of kids I see on two or three simultaneous medications grows exponentially with each passing year. According to IMS Health, the pharmaceutical industry's equivalent of the Nielsen ratings service, the use of Prozac-like drugs for children was up 74 percent between 1995 and 1999. During the same period, the use of mood stabilizers, not including lithium, rose by 4,000 percent, and prescriptions for new antipsychotic medications like risperdal have grown by nearly 300 percent. According to DEA statistics, production of Ritalin increased by over 700 percent between 1990 and 1998.*

To my way of thinking and those of many of my friends and colleagues, these facts, if true, are completely unacceptable. Something is going very wrong here that must be changed. How did these kind of drugs become the primary path for so many children? There just must be a better way.

– James B LeVine, Ph.D.
Honolulu, Hawaii

Introduction

Great child rearing is a rapidly diminishing art, yet it need not be. We can begin to revive the art of fine parenting by doing just two things:

- ✦ Remembering that parenting is a privilege.
- ✦ Rediscovering the importance of play.

In order to regard parenting as a privilege, a mother or father must deeply respect the idea that children—not parents—are the ultimate arbiters of their own development. Children will accept our guidance and follow our suggestions if we prove ourselves worthy of their trust. We will demonstrate and earn this trust if we adopt a child-centered parenting approach instead of a parent-centered approach.

What is child-centered parenting? It's parenting that is done with the child's own preferences, learning style, and unique personality foremost in mind.

As for the importance of play, children were designed by nature to learn and grow best through play. Personally, I am fascinated by play. I like to call myself a participant, advocate, and scientist of play.

At the heart of all play is a passion for living. Children know this instinctively; it's we adults who have somehow lost sight of this truth and need to regain it.

This book is intended to be a helpful tool for you. I hope

it will assist you in looking at the world differently than you have up to this point. It may challenge your preconceptions, and in so doing reveal to you where these are on the scale between loosely held opinions and rock-solid premises.

Presumably you've picked up this book to browse because you're seeking some new ideas or confirmation of your current point of view. Perhaps you'll strongly disagree or happily find validation. Whatever the case, I hope you'll be challenged to improve your parenting.

PARENTING IS NOW MAINLY DONE BY SUBSTITUTES

These are challenging times for parents. As our culture adapts to meet a new era, traditional parenting methods are giving way to new forms. In the big picture, the American family is continuing its transformation from a large, extended network that parented by community to a small, subnuclear household that parents through substitutes. These parenting stand-ins may be teachers, baby-sitters, daycare providers, school psychologists, pediatric psychiatrists, before-school and after-school programs, and of course television, computer games, and the Internet.

Such surrogate parents are providing a flood of information to our children that influences them both positively and negatively, too often without the knowledge—let alone the direct consent—of parents themselves. In fact, the delegation of responsibility has gone so far that school systems and social service agencies are now beginning to assert legal challenges to parental authority. Apparently some parental substitutes are beginning to see themselves as having a responsibility for the upbringing of children that is equal to or even greater than that of the parents. In some cases, they may be right.

INTRODUCTION

THE TREND TO SMALLER FAMILIES AND SINGLE PARENTHOOD

The proportion of single-parent families continues to increase relative to all families. To date, about three in every ten families has only one parent. This is largely an involuntary result of the high divorce rate in a nation in which one of every two marriages fails, and partly due to other causes such as an increase in the popularity of single parenting by choice. Whatever the reason, for the past fifteen years this trend has been accelerating until it has reached the rate of about one-half of a percent per year. Traditional two-parent families that stay together are also joining the trend toward smaller families by having fewer children.

SMALLER ISN'T NECESSARILY BETTER

This cultural transformation is not proving beneficial for children. In fact, many observers see serious problems with the way today's children are being brought up. They cite as evidence any number of social problems that involve young people— from declining math and reading scores and pervasive boredom to violence, drug abuse, suicide, and murder. One of the most disturbing statistics is that between eight and twelve million young school children in the U.S. are probably being managed by prescription drugs—given behavior-modification medication mandated by school systems to calm down their "childish" behavior so that they can better focus on classroom tasks (extrapolations of Diller, INCB, Merrow Report, Parry).

GOOD PARENTING CAN STILL BE ACHIEVED

Although these demographic changes haven't happened overnight, we can see that, over the span of a single generation, parenting styles and child-rearing practices have deteriorated

3

to the point where the effects are now showing up as alarming statistics. In light of this, one could speculate that it's no longer possible to give children the kind of upbringing we enjoyed just a generation ago. Yet I believe that a good upbringing is still very possible, different though it may have to be to suit today's family situations.

There is more to good parenting than meets the eye, especially in our rapidly changing world. Certainly there is much more to raising children than providing for their basic needs: food, clothing, shelter, moral guidance, and medical attention. Crucially, there is much to understand about the nature of children—who they are, what they need, and how they develop—so that their upbringing can proceed effectively.

NEW INFORMATION ABOUT CHILDREN

We can have no set of absolutes, for too much remains to be discovered about how children develop. But in the past decade alone, major breakthroughs in neurology have uncovered the fact that, quite early in life, children have a far greater capacity to learn than has ever been thought. These discoveries show that children's brains have a tremendous capacity to be enriched, and that they probably need more enrichment than they are typically receiving. And we now know that learning is far more effective when it is initiated and fulfilled by the child through play.

SELECTING GOOD PARENTAL SUBSTITUTES IS CRUCIAL

Parents need not know everything there is to know about children in order to practice good parenting. However, a fundamental knowledge of the basics can make parenting easier—and far better than proceeding without any insight. Since the

INTRODUCTION

use of substitute parenting is growing and parental authority is being increasingly delegated, it is now more important than ever that parents master the selection and use of good programs, services, and products. This knowledgeable selection needs to happen if parents are to govern their children's upbringing effectively. In this way, parents can be more aware of any changes occurring in their children as a result of experiences outside the home—experiences in which the information and lessons they are exposed to cannot be directly witnessed by the parents.

WHY TODAY'S PARENTS NEED TO LEARN MORE ABOUT PARENTING

Besides the fact that times are changing, parents of today have other compelling reasons to learn more about parenting: First, babies don't come with instruction manuals. It is one of mankind's greatest ironies that even the simplest household appliance comes with diagrams and illustrated instructions for use, often in several languages, with cautionary warning statements, but have a baby and you're on your own. This lack of instruction for parents is both a freedom and a curse. While there is no shortage of reference material on the subject of raising children, and one can easily source advice from friends, neighbors, and relatives, no parenting standards exist that can be pointed to with any unanimity as being the ideal.

Parenting values and methods are regarded as being something like art or beauty—that is to say, subjective: truth lies in the eye of the beholder. It may be liberating that any individual parent can do nearly anything with his or her children. But it is also disquieting to consider the damage that can be done by the well-intentioned but uninformed,

5

and to remember that—unless the damage is obvious and considerable—such parents will not be held accountable to any law or standard. It is precisely because we lack accountability requirements that parents need to learn as much as they can, so as to give their children the best upbringing possible and avoid any unintended consequences.

I say this because nature is forgiving as to how and when we convey to children the information we think they need to absorb, but the results later in the child's life may not be. That's why having a big-picture grasp of the content, source, and effectiveness of the flow of information from the outside world is so important to parents as responsible overseers of their children's upbringing.

EXTENDED FAMILIES ARE NO MORE

Another reason why today's mothers and fathers need to learn more about good parenting is that most of us no longer have the resource of a large extended family—grandparents, aunties, uncles, cousins, many brothers and sisters, long-term friends, and caring neighbors—to call upon. Some fragments of these resources remain, to be sure, but for a whole host of reasons most of them are no longer available.

Coincident with this has been the sexual revolution. As a result of feminism, great numbers of women in the United States have, in order to work outside the home, given up much of their traditional role as family leader in the upbringing of children. Included in the earlier "familyhood" and "motherhood" resources were nearly all the upbringing skills that our society had accumulated over time. Parents of prior generations not only had daily lessons in how to parent but also a daily apprenticeship. Most parents today have had no

INTRODUCTION

access to such training and practice. They did not get it at home and they did not get it in the classroom.

No parental training courses are required in schools. There are many books on the subject for do-it-yourselfers, but by and large, the seeking out of training is left to the initiative of the parent. Although I was not able to find any factual statistics on the matter, my suspicions are that few parents go very far in the search. There are reasons for this we can imagine: cost, lack of time, higher priorities elsewhere, bewilderment at too many choices offered by disagreeing professionals and/or advocates, denial, ignorance, and lack of concern. In addition, there are no direct penalties for poor or incompetent parenting.

Our society allows for broad latitude in overall upbringing supervision. This permissiveness is remarkable in the context of so many restrictions placed on behaviors of much less significance; for example, driving a motor vehicle. No test of parenting skills comparable to a driver's license exam is required in order for one to undertake parenting. All can parent, from the most to the least competent.

PARENTING IS LIFE'S MOST IMPORTANT RESPONSIBILITY

Yet another reason why today's parents need to learn more about parenting is that it is arguably the most important responsibility that any person can have in this life. I believe that there is no more important factor in the future of the human race than the quality of its people, and a direct relationship exists between the quality of upbringing and the quality of life. The quality of upbringing can be equated to the quality of parenting.

Parenting is such an important responsibility that it's a puzzlement why there is no parental accountability for success

THE PRIVILEGE OF PARENTING

or failure. The remarkable thing is how well parents do at parenting despite their lack of training and the dearth of traditional family support. Apparently love, good intentions, good judgment, reasonable intelligence, resourcefulness, instincts, family loyalty, responsibility, moral courage, and common sense can still go a long way to solving many problems. And while we're on the subject of remarkable parenting, it is usually mothering for which we have mainly to be thankful. This certainly is true in my own case.

Just what is the best way to bring up a child? Of course there is neither just one right way nor one preferred way, but we do have some solid principles to follow. In this book, I will go into the nature of children before I proceed to their parenting and upbringing. After presenting some of the latest research findings about child development, I'll offer you numerous suggestions and resources to assist you in carrying out your responsibilities as a parent.

I sincerely hope that the sharing of these ideas will help my readers find their way with confidence in an increasingly complex and dangerously uncertain world.

CHAPTER 1

Does *U*pbringing Matter?

Does one's upbringing matter? "Of course," some of you will say, "sure it does. Upbringing is critical. What kind of question is that?" Others will say, "No, no, no. It doesn't matter at all. Mary had a rotten childhood, and look what happened. She turned out fantastically, so obviously her upbringing had little effect on her."

Who's right and who's wrong? Well, before we go any further, I had better tell you where I stand on the issue. This is not a book that will question whether upbringing matters or not, nor is it a social science textbook. My position stems unequivocally from the assumption that one's upbringing does matter a great deal, period. That's my central premise because, through observing my own children as well as many others for more than three decades, I have seen the connection — the clear relationship between cause and effect, input and output, action and reaction, and the eventual outcomes that result.

Human nature is complex. We have no rules to follow that will guarantee certain behaviors, nor are the situations in which we find ourselves always straightforward, governed by simple principles or factors. Bearing this in mind, our individual childhood experiences will still affect our behavior. Some may look at what is in front of them and use the lessons they learned as children to deal with it. Others may regard an identical circumstance and rebel against their parents' values

CHAPTER ONE

in order to move through it. Both scenarios are possible, because our reactions to life situations are affected by a multitude of internal and external variables. An individual's upbringing is but one of these variables, yet I believe it to be the most important one.

WHAT IS UPBRINGING?

So what is upbringing? How am I defining it? I attribute a more comprehensive meaning to the term than is common, because I see upbringing as a deliberate process full of particulars—the sum total of all influences upon our childhood. It's important to make the distinction that upbringing is not any one action, but many actions strung together over a period of years.

Upbringing clearly implies intentional parental influence, or what I'll call the "input" actions that are taken by a parent to guide a child toward an intended outcome. I also think upbringing can be seen as an unintentional, "default input." In other words, the many things that parents do and don't do, intend and don't intend, all result in upbringing inputs to a child. For example, a parent may not intend to pass along a smoking habit. But if that parent smokes in front of a child, the child will more than likely be influenced to smoke when the opportunity arises. Or if a child witnesses how an adult takes no action in the face of some recurring situation, "no action" is the take-home message the child will learn.

PARENTING IS MENTORING

A key element in my definition of upbringing is parenting. What is parenting? Other than holding its primary meaning

10

as the action of originating the life of a child, I believe that parenting, in the context of upbringing, is closest to mentoring. Mentoring, in turn, is guidance activity conducted by a trusted and experienced person whose goal is the advancement and welfare of the person being mentored. So, in this sense, a parent can be likened to a teacher, a tutor, or a coach. But a parent is also much more than a mentor, because of the close, personal nature of the relationship a parent shares with a child. Parental motives in guiding children are far more complex than merely sublimating all other concerns to the welfare of the child.

PARENTING IS ALSO MENTORING BY SUBSTITUTES

I am also using the term parenting as mentoring in a broader sense. A large part of raising children is their "parenting" by designated individuals who act as parental substitutes, or substitutes that are animate, inanimate, and even virtual, i.e., programs, services, and products provided by strangers who are external to the home environment. In such cases, parental authority to mentor the child has been deliberately delegated to these stand-ins by the birth parents or legal guardians.

I want to highlight the fact that all forms of substitution are delegations of responsibility. Parents need always to be aware that, any time a child's upbringing has been temporarily delegated to a surrogate, for that period of time the substitute has complete mentoring responsibility in the child's upbringing. I bring this to your attention because I think this transfer of trust and responsibility is frequently taken too lightly by all concerned. Forgive me, then, if I give you frequent reminders of this fact.

CHAPTER ONE

WHAT IS A CHILD?

> *Neither in environment nor in heredity can I find the*
> *exact instrument that fashioned me, the anonymous*
> *roller that passed upon my life a certain intricate*
> *watermark whose unique design becomes visible*
> *when the lamp of art is made to shine through life's*
> *foolscap.*
>
> – Vladimir Nabokov, *Speak, Memory*

I want to communicate my views to you with clarity in order for you to understand why I take the positions I do. So, while we're defining terms, I may as well briefly touch on my definition of a child.

Other than being (1) your genetic progeny, a child is (2) a reflection of the influence of the settings in which she finds herself and (3) her own inherent, unique character. I see children as fresh, clean slates, as empty vessels who are highly impressionable. In this state in which they know almost nothing and believe almost everything, they are both wonderfully and horribly vulnerable to all influences.

If you have trouble remembering what it was like to be a child, imagine being perpetually at a magic show where every trick is accepted as reality. When you see the magician sawing the subject in half, you accept it as fact. When you see rabbits jumping out of thin air, you wonder why everyone around you is applauding in amazement because it looks perfectly normal to you. And when you see a person floating without any apparent support, you accept levitation without question.

Everyone knows that children are open to the world around them and everything in it. They are less prejudicial than adults and less judgmental of the events that occur in their surroundings. They have the fearlessness of naiveté. Because they have so little history to which they can compare the things they see, they accept nearly everything as reality. Compare this to your adult attitude, in which just the opposite is quite clearly understood: the idea that much of what you see before you is an illusion to be distrusted and investigated. This "virtual" take on life is especially true for those of us who watch a lot of television.

As Eleanor Roosevelt once said, "Because they have so little experience, children must rely on imagination." Children's imaginations, compared to those of adults, enjoy much more freedom. For example, gravity is a flexible concept to a child, not an absolute natural law. The state of being naïve — of having a meager store of knowledge, experience, or judgment, combined with high vulnerability and impressionability — makes children what they are.

WHY CHILDREN NEED PARENTING

Children need parents to give them the wider perspective they sorely lack. During the early years of childhood, we accept that our children have only the narrowest base of information upon which to make good judgments. We may find this innocence endearing for a time, as indeed it is. Yet, as time goes on, our attitude of indulgence may change to impatience as we witness our children blundering into easily avoidable problems. Then the question becomes: How long can we stand for our children to be so naive?

CHAPTER ONE

PARENTS ARE HELD ACCOUNTABLE FOR HOW THEIR KIDS TURN OUT

In our society, parents are expected to exert control over their children's childhood influences and experiences, impossible though this may be.

When someone says, "He had a wonderful upbringing," we may all know that this is just a pleasantry, a generality that lacks the specific meaning we're attributing to upbringing here. However, we're also uncomfortably aware that the world will ultimately hold us responsible for the kinds of adults our children become. For, when our children are grown men and women, their value judgments, the activities in which they engage, and the life choices they make (both wise and unwise) will be seen as direct results of earlier choices *we* made in their upbringing.

Upbringing implies following an overall strategy and employing consistent tactics. Such consistency may not be present in all cases, for child-rearing patterns vary considerably from parent to parent. However, if we're inevitably going to be held responsible for how our children turn out, then I think it behooves us to devise a strategy of upbringing. In this way we can be more likely to merit the world's praise and avoid its censure. This book will give you methodical advice on creating or improving that master strategy.

Now that we've come to a better understanding of terms, we can go on. This book isn't made up of traditional parenting wisdom, for our times call for new wisdom. I hope I've given you at least a preliminary understanding of my purpose, so that you can better understand the many nontraditional statements and suggestions to follow.

SELECTING AND DELEGATING TO PARENTAL SUBSTITUTES

Selecting the right people, programs, services, and products to act as parenting substitutes for your children is one of your most important duties as a parent, and is crucial to the strategy we touched on earlier. If you're an experienced parent, you've been doing the best you can for years; if you're a new parent, you've already got a small taste of the effort this requires; and if you're a parent-to-be, you're probably looking ahead to this responsibility with some trepidation.

Whatever your situation, you know that your selections will play a significant role in shaping your children's future. The individuals and other resources that you select to provide these services can be critically important, and of course you also know that the devil is in the details: timing and scheduling these programs, while matching the products and services to your children's interests and temperaments, is absolutely crucial. Therefore the selection process may not be easy. Here are some simple truths:

1. Knowledge is power. To do your parenting job well, you need to make some basic comparisons in order to make good choices. Each program, service, and product takes time to research—time that you may have precious little of.

2. A large and ever-growing number of children's programs, services, and products exist from which to select, but these may be challenging for you to discover, because . . .

3. Good consumer information is lacking for many of these programs. Advertising is expensive, and may be more costly than some smaller organizations can afford. We

CHAPTER ONE

have no child services industry to speak of, just non-cohesive programs, services, and products. The federal government can provide no more than minimal information and consumer-protection regulations concerning these providers. The consumer-information industry, as a whole, is fragmented and imperfect.

4. The providers themselves aren't necessarily the best people to evaluate the quality of their own offerings. No matter how good they are, they have a built-in credibility problem. How many consumer advertisements or infomercials do you believe without question? It's still a caveat emptor (let the buyer beware) world out there. Besides, even the most competent providers and programs may not be appropriate for your children at their stage of development.

Knowing all that, you must still make some choices. Not selecting at least a few services for your children is not an option. You have to select, no matter what, if you're going to live in this society. Your children have to go to school somewhere, even if at home. They have to eat, learn, wear clothes, and engage in activities every day.

If you feel that, as a consumer, you have insufficient information at the time that you need to make a choice, you must still do your best to choose the optimal situation for your child. You must make selections, even if by default. Certainly "no choice" is one option, but need I remind you that "no choice" *is* a choice, and one with real consequences? So consider the "no choice" option with the same care you would give to any other.

16

WHAT THIS GUIDEBOOK CAN GIVE YOU

Making the process of selecting children's programs, services, and products simpler for you as a consumer and more helpful to your children is the goal of this guidebook. The following are some of the benefits I intend for you to receive. You'll get a better feel for:

✦ How to prioritize the selection process for your children. I'll suggest that you take a "program follows function" approach to help your children match their activities to their own temperament, character, and interests.

✦ How to search for programs, services and products. I'll suggest a "seek and connect" method. Many services available to children aren't well publicized, so seeking and finding is important. Good programs will probably not find *you*, but you can learn how to find *them*.

✦ The scope of what's out there and available. I'll suggest that you follow a "forest first, then the trees" approach, to put the odds in favor of your finding better selections. Seeing many of these services at one time in this book will give you an overview to help you first consider all the sources, then start to narrow them down intelligently.

✦ How to evaluate a program, service, or product—in effect, how to be a better comparison shopper. I'll suggest that you "get an attitude" . . . a mental attitude with which to arm yourself. The attitude will lead to healthy questions for you to ask yourself, your children, and the potential providers, to evaluate how well their offerings will fit your

CHAPTER ONE

children's needs. You'll learn to determine the limitations of different choices, such as participant age, expected costs, and time needed to master the activity.

A SUMMARY OF CHAPTER ONE

My list of good parenting skills for our time can be summed up as follows:

+ Understanding who your children are, including their genetic base and unique character.

+ Developing a master strategy and consistent tactics to enhance their development over time.

+ Selecting programs, products, and services to help you wisely delegate your responsibility so that you can fulfill these strategies and tactics.

+ Having an effective overview so that you can monitor and manage the upbringing process.

At the heart of good parenting is a very challenging mentoring process. Most parents come to the job untrained and must learn as they go along; also, consumer information about parental substitutes is seriously lacking.

Parents need to be highly aware that children are very different from adults. This is simultaneously their greatest charm and their most serious vulnerability.

ASSIGNMENT FOR CHAPTER ONE

Sit down with a pen and paper and write as many one-sentence definitions of parenting as you can. Stop when you can't think of any more. You should probably have from three to six definitions.

DOES UPBRINGING MATTER?

Next, go through the list and identify where you think these definitions came from, e.g., from the way your parents raised you, from ideas you may have borrowed from your relatives or friends, or from depictions of parenthood you may have seen in movies or on television.

Finally, define your ideal parenting model. You can identify a definition already described by you in this exercise, modify one of your definitions, or come up with a new idea that most closely fits the ideal. Summarize this as succinctly as possible.

Extra credit: Try to define where you were trained to be a parent. What skills did you learn, and from what source?

CHAPTER 2

The Problem with Preconceptions

Unless you're never home or a very uninvolved parent, your children will know everything that you are: every attitude, every foible, and every prejudice. By everything, I mean warts and all. The thing of it is, you don't have to say anything directly to them. Your essence will simply permeate their consciousness. How does this happen? Well, in the case of birth parents, they do have your genes! Thus, they have all of your potential—for the good and the not so good.

Besides that, your children have eagle eyes. They watch everything you do, see everything you are, and will eventually uncover anything you try to hide. They may not even be speaking yet, but they understand everything you say, with powers mankind has yet to fully understand. They also have a perfect understanding of your tone, your body language, and your facial expressions. (My own children would start crying if they sensed I was walking angrily!)

Kids know how much you love them, or how little. They know whether you're fair, and just how fair you are. They know when you're too self-absorbed and selfish. You may not notice any of this now, but take the time for a careful look and you'll be amazed and humbled. Give your children much more credit than you ordinarily do. After all, they're chips off the old block.

Hear this from someone who's been there. You might want to start taking stock of your outdated habits and viewpoints now, and begin to work on a personal spring cleaning so you won't have the shock of seeing your bad habits or prejudices staring back at you in the form of your children.

ELIMINATE FAULTS TO AVOID PASSING THEM ALONG

Do you like everything about yourself? Are you 100 percent behind all your beliefs? Are you proud of your positions? I hope so. But if you have any self-doubts, then you probably need to do some repair work. Take me seriously on this: you are your children's role model for everything. Work with this fact and remember it well, because there's no escaping it for the rest of your life. Your children mirror you; it's as simple as that. If you need to do a few revisions, jettison some of your broad sweeping generalizations. Eliminate some irrational choices. Shelve some of those phrases that seem to spring to your lips every time things don't go well. And leave the sailor talk out of your vocabulary unless you want to hear it come back to you.

YOUR CHILDREN WILL ASSIMILATE YOUR WORLDVIEW

> *And that's the world in a nutshell—an appropriate receptacle.*
>
> – Stan Dunn

What are your own general preconceptions about life? Are you afraid of the world? Are you an optimist or a pessimist?

CHAPTER TWO

Are people in the world basically good or basically bad? Give yourself a checkup. Ask yourself if we need more people in the world who share your belief system. Ask yourself what the consequences of these beliefs would be over a lifetime. Parenthood provides an opportunity to review and to clean your own house—before, during, and after being cloned by your kids.

CHILDREN ARE DIFFERENT FROM GROWNUPS

My mother had a great deal of trouble with me, but I think she enjoyed it.

– Mark Twain

How many times have you heard this old saying, or something like it? *God made kids so cute and lovable because if they weren't, everyone would hate them and the human race would probably have vanished long ago?* Does this sentiment ring true to you? If you're a parent-to-be or novice parent, do you have preconceptions about children? What are you bringing to the table in the way of expectations?

Small children are not the same as you and me. They don't speak intelligibly, they don't employ what we know as reason, and they have little tact or grace about them. When they get upset, "keep it mellow" is not a concept that guides their behavior. They are rough around the edges and absolutely honest. Little children follow no rules because they don't know any. They are tiny bulls in a china shop. They are tyrannical. They employ almost no analytical powers—just primal instincts. They have no shame, no preconceptions, and no sense of restraint.

Children never hesitate to employ all the tools at their

THE PROBLEM WITH PRECONCEPTIONS

disposal, such as a strong voice, volcanic bursts of emotion, and total subjectivity. They are self-centered in the truest sense of the word, and bent on controlling whomever is nearby to get their needs met. But here's the interesting part. It's reported that the average child laughs from 200 to 400 times a day. Are they having a whale of a time? Absolutely!

On the other side of this equation stand you and your mate. Your children may be virtually free of constraints, but you aren't. You have a raft of riveted beliefs and unshakeable ways. You are decidedly reasonable. You have grace and sensitivity. Your feathers get ruffled easily when someone breaks the rules. You have a life history, and highly skilled powers of observation to modify your behavior. Freud would be proud of your analytical skills. Are *you* having any fun? Well . . . you laugh on average a mere fifteen times a day and, according to Juliet Schor in *Overworked America*, if you're a working adult you average only 2.5 hours of free time each day. What's wrong with this picture?

When you don the cloak of parenting, will you adjust to these realities, adapt, and thrive? Knowing about them is one thing; living with them is another. Being around children can certainly be enjoyable. On the other hand, as roommates they may be your worst nightmare. Are you parents-to-be ready for this? You and your children will have contrasting viewpoints and behavior. Remember that they will sense your attitudes about these differences. First they'll sense them, then they'll absorb them, and finally they'll mimic them. Following that, they may adopt, discard, or ridicule them.

Kids are uncannily good mimics. They'll try you on like a new pair of shoes, but discard you soon after if they sense it's a poor fit. If you don't care for the idea of being spoofed by

23

CHAPTER TWO

your own children, it might be good to review your attitudes and your preconceptions in private before displaying them to your young ones, and then take steps to modify any that no longer fit. And while you're at it, laugh a little!

THERE ARE NO SUREFIRE METHODS OF INFLUENCE

Children are hard to figure out. You can never be certain what's motivating them, how much they see, or how much they understand about what's going on around them. You may think you can, but that's likely your ego talking. If you already have kids, then you know one thing for certain: Your children will decide what, when, and whom they are influenced by.

Those of us with kids have tried and probably failed miserably at cajoling our youngsters to finish their peas, pick up their mess, or brush their teeth if they're resisting. What other tactics do we employ? Some of us try humor or flattery; others try raising our voices; and still others attempt to shame the tykes using sarcasm. Some of us may even use an old-fashioned spanking to get our point across, although that does more harm than good.

There's the carrot-and-stick approach, as in tantalizing the kids with something they want, and its opposite: motivation by threatening to take privileges away. Then there's the silent approach: refusing to speak or do anything interactive with the kids. There's the sending them-to-their-room or time-out approach (all too frequently combined with meal deprivation). There's also emotional harassment, like the use of excessive drama.

We all have our favorite tactics that we know are ineffectual but still practice, mainly because they're so ingrained in us from our own childhood. When all else fails, we invoke parental privilege and throw a tantrum ourselves, which can take any number of forms . . . yelling, sulking, nagging, or grouchiness, none of which make us feel very good.

YOU CAN'T CONTROL CHILDREN

My parents put a live teddy bear in my crib.

– Woody Allen

The next time your child throws a tantrum, remember that he's actually being smart: he's learned that the likelihood of getting his way by tantrum is 95 percent or better. So stay calm and resist the knee-jerk impulse to fight back. Resist it with all your might.

Now repeat after me: *I cannot control my children. I will not outsmart my children. I will not outthink my children. I won't make my daughter obedient. I won't succeed at planning my son's future. I will fail at picking my daughter's friends. I'll fail miserably in getting my son interested in what I'm interested in, and later on my ship will go down if I try to pick a wife for him. I cannot make my children become good doctors, lawyers, or even productive citizens. I can't finish reading a book for my daughter. And I can't eat my son's lima beans and make him strong and powerful. I am not without influence, but I have no power to control my children's future. I will accept this and move on. If I find myself feeling resentful, I'll remember that I'm not likely to outlive my progeny. So I'll try a different tack: I'll live my own life with gusto and be happy. I'll follow my own star. If there's value in who I am, my children will see it, but I won't be too disappointed if they don't follow in my footsteps. Whatever I do, I'll give up any ideas about controlling my children. And the sooner I resolve to do this, the better.*

CHAPTER TWO

IT'S NATURAL TO HAVE EXPECTATIONS FOR YOUR CHILDREN

There was a time when we expected nothing of children but obedience, as opposed to the present, when we expect everything of them but obedience.

— Anatole Broyard

All these words of wisdom notwithstanding, what do you want for your children? A multitude of things, probably. Joseph Kennedy, Sr., wanted his son John to be president after John's older brother, Joseph Jr., tragically passed away. Joe Kennedy got his wish; why shouldn't you get yours? If you're like me, you've thought about this question since the time your children were born. It's perfectly natural to do this, since you want the best for your children. You want them to enjoy good health, success, material comfort, fulfillment, contentment, and happiness. You're not alone in this; we all share these aspirations. Yet hopes, desires, and good wishes are one thing; serious expectations are another.

But how can expectations be anything but serious, you ask? Let's talk about that.

BRING ALL YOUR EXPECTATIONS OUT IN THE OPEN, THEN KEEP THEM UNDER CONTROL

Beware the peril of nurturing expectations about your children's future. This is treacherous ground. If you're brimming with hope for their eventual careers as astronauts or U.S. presidents, you'd better give yourself a good talking to. Take it from a parent who knows. Let go of your attachment to any future scenario for your kids, because unfulfilled expectations can be a cause of serious troubles. The key factor will be your own attitude about your thwarted expectations. Will

26

you be bitterly disappointed? Will your ego be shattered? Will your children go down in your esteem? Will you withdraw some amount of the love you have for them?

Ask yourself to what extent you would intervene to make your wishes come true. Aspirations have a way of simmering below the surface before they become overt, and at this subconscious level your feelings may come out subtly in your words and actions.

The problem isn't that we have expectations. It's natural to have dreams for our children; this is an expression of our love for them. The problems arise when our visions become unrealistic. So be careful with expectations. Keep them light, and if you sense that your personal agenda regarding your children is creating tension within your family, discuss your feelings with everyone concerned. This kind of open communication should go a long way toward diffusing anger or resentment.

YOU NEEDN'T TEACH YOUR CHILDREN EVERYTHING

Infants only seem to be blank slates. Actually they come with many skills, behaviors, and preferences already hardwired— some obvious, some just being discovered, and many yet to be discovered. Crying is one example, sucking another, and cuddling still another. These are instinctive behaviors that you as parent don't need to teach. (Hallelujah! Can you imagine how hard it would be? My babies would have starved if they'd depended upon me to teach them to take a bottle!)

Nature has cut parents a break by engineering babies with their fundamental skills built in. So you can relax a little. You needn't worry about teaching your kids to play, explore, touch, taste, push, eat, watch, listen, or concentrate—babies

CHAPTER TWO

are born with all of the senses and skills available to mankind. It's amazing. None of this needs to be taught by anyone. It just happens miraculously.

DEVELOPING A MANAGEMENT STYLE

The reason grandparents and grandchildren get along so well is that they have a common enemy.

– Sam Levenson

How do you treat your boss at work? Are you usually on your best behavior? Is there an element of heightened respect—a good flow of communication based on the mutual need for a satisfactory working relationship? Do you dwell on past mistakes, or concentrate on improvements and going forward?

Day by day, your parental role is to be both the good guy and the bad guy to your child, much as your boss is to you. When you have time and are in top form, you'll find it easy to excel at positive mentoring. But when your children make mistakes, break the rules, and do "bad" things, your role gets much more challenging. The style you adopt to manage and get along with your children is critically important to their upbringing. You may already be painfully aware of this. The way you approach children should be as considerate as the way you relate to other adults. In fact, the phrase "Handle them with kid gloves" should always inform your relationships with your kids.

We've already covered the fact that you can't directly persuade your children to think or to do anything, and I've done my best to deflate your enterprising expectations for their future. Yet I've also made the point that children are very observant of what you do, what you believe, what you value, and what your body language and tone of voice communicate. Your children will be managed by watching you over a long period of time, not by your immediate directives in the short term. Clearly, your children are being influenced in the manner that holds greatest credibility for them.

CHILDREN RESPOND TO WHAT YOU DO, NOT WHAT YOU SAY

Children have marvelous powers of discrimination. They can tune out your "spin" on situations — those things you say (but may not do) to influence their behavior. They pay attention to what you do, not what you say. So the sum total of everything you communicate to your children can be found in your daily lifestyle. If you're having problems with your progeny, this is an area you should focus on.

Pay close attention to consistency here. "Do as I say and not as I do" doesn't work in the majority of cases. Your children are learning how you manage your life by observing you in many situations. You may not be aware that you're teaching them this way, but you should be. This kind of learning has an impact on a whole array of childish behaviors. Your kids will be alert to inconsistencies between the way you ask them to handle things and the way you've handled the very same things over a long period of time.

Inconsistencies confuse children, especially when you want them to take a certain course that they haven't witnessed *you* taking. If you meet with resistance in your efforts to persuade your child of something, this is probably why. For example, the way you treat every stranger that comes into the view and earshot of your children will be closely noted. If you're consistently cheerful and pleasant, your children will conclude that this behavior is appropriate for them in similar

29

CHAPTER TWO

circumstances. If you instruct them to be wary of strangers, they'll see the inconsistency and be puzzled. If they're really confused, they'll be more likely to follow your long-term example than your now-and-then advice.

YOU WON'T KNOW HOW YOU'VE DONE TILL YOU'RE DONE

Besides having the necessary base of knowledge, masterful parenting consists of doing everything necessary to get the job done: managing, facilitating, teaching, legislating, adjudicating, gatekeeping, begging, borrowing, or stealing, and a whole lot more. Patience, resourcefulness, and flexibility are important skills to possess, along with nimbleness, endurance, and keen awareness. But, in the long run, humility is probably the most important trait.

The test of masterful parenthood will not be whether you're still standing with your wits intact at the end of the day, having performed a thousand different tasks and worn two dozen different hats. No, the real test will be how well your children will have turned out when your role as parent has diminished. Parenthood is a complex, interactive process, and unfortunately you can't immediately know how well you're doing. For much of the time, you'll be operating in the dark.

IN THE MEANTIME, HOW CAN YOU TAKE YOUR BEST GUESS?

Knowing how well you're doing as you proceed would be valuable, if only you could figure out how to do it. If you have had no training in parenting and are depending upon on-the-job instruction, it could be especially important. You can't assume that you'll do well just because you are who you are. So how can this knowledge be achieved?

30

■ Find Your Humility

The first thing you need is a large measure of humility. Having an ample amount will take the edge off your commanding or controlling attitude, and you'll move to a higher level of consciousness about the impact your behavior has upon your children. You need to accept that though your heart may be in the right place, you might not have all the skills necessary to safely steer your children's lives through all the challenges of their upbringing. However, you *are* willing to keep your eyes and ears open, and proceed with an open mind. On the other side of humility lies confidence. Be humble in your approach, but not so humble that you lose trust in your own ability; first to see, then to believe that the emperor has no clothes.

■ Build a Support Team

The second thing you need is a support team. The benefit of more eyes and ears to supplement your observations about your child can be invaluable. If it isn't practical or desirable to have your extended family or your own nuclear family help you raise your children, then you're going to have to run a parentocracy centered largely around your work schedule, with the least amount possible of negative impact upon your children. If you're going to run a parentocracy, at least you should strive to be a benevolent dictator.

By support team, I mean relatives, doctors, specialists, teachers, nannies, au pairs, baby-sitters, neighbors, and friends. These people are valuable resources that you should approach frequently for a second opinion about what you're observing.

The other side of this is the potential problem of delegating too much of your responsibility. Delegation needs to be doled

CHAPTER TWO

out very conservatively, with you fully realizing that any number of parenting duties simply *cannot* be delegated. A good course of action is to prepare for emergencies of all kinds, and then communicate these emergency plans to your substitutes.

■ Be Wary of All Advice

Thirdly, you need to form the proper attitude about working with your support team. Be wary of all advice — especially expert advice. Keep an open mind, but don't be too taken in by credentials of any kind. Whenever anyone offers advice, try to separate fact from opinion, and then keep opinion at arm's length. Remember that the primary value your team has for you is that of being your eyes and ears in your absence. You alone have the global view of your child's upbringing.

■ Trust Your Child

Finally, give your child as much respect and trust as you can possibly muster. Respect, from your point of view, should mean observing in an almost clinical, scientifically objective way your child's skills, preferences, and limitations. After you observe, and confirm your observations, work with your findings instead of fighting them. Pay particular attention to your child's learning processes, and the tools she uses. If your child has musical curiosity, for example, enable her to explore the possibilities and *stay out of the way while she experiments with it.* Listen carefully to what she says and does about it. Don't be too quick to get involved. Don't hire a music teacher of a specific instrument who will impose a strict regimen.

32

Working with the findings you've made, based upon your child's patterns, is an entirely different approach than imposing your ideas or those of anyone else from the outside. For example, you should give priority to getting your child's questions answered before your own and before those that come from others, including your support team. Answers to questions that she herself has posed are the most valuable to your child.

HOW TO CHOOSE FOR YOUR CHILDREN

In her book *It Takes a Village*, Hillary Clinton made the point that we don't bring up our children alone. We are quite dependent upon the world around us—our community and our nation—to give us a helping hand. This is probably true in the case of your own family. The question is not whether you'll use the parental surrogates found in the world around us, but which ones, how many, and when.

Why will you choose the particular substitutes that you do? Whenever you (1) feel like buying a toy; (2) are persuaded to do so by your child; or (3) are manipulated into doing so by an impending birthday or holiday event, you must know that there are numerous forces pushing you to make that purchase. The same is true, although to a lesser extent, with children's programs and services. In addition to the obvious urging of your child and of the commercial world, some of these forces are self-generated—they are your background and experiences. After some practice, masterful parents learn to sort through all of these voices and make the right choices. Here are some things to keep in mind when you find yourself there.

CHAPTER TWO

■ It's Your Job to Schedule the Majority of Your Child's Time

Children are similar to machines that are always on. Unlike an appliance with an ON/OFF switch, a child's time must be accounted for every moment, every hour, every day, every week, and every year for the eighteen or more years that they are in your care. You certainly don't need to coexperience every one of those moments with your child, but you do need to at least loosely schedule the majority of them. That is, in the best interests of your child, you should spend the time and effort necessary to oversee those moments.

■ Which Programs, Services, and Products Will You Select?

The surrogates you choose will have an effect on your children. They won't just occupy space and time. You need to be thinking about these effects, because some of them may not be desirable.

One way to think about the effects is to recall our earlier discussion about children and play. To reiterate, children see the world best through their most important function: play. Their play model operates best when they are allowed enough time and space to freely explore, interact with, and integrate their experience of whatever they're playing with. So the most important question becomes this: *Does the program, service, or product under consideration enable my child to play effectively?* That is, will it allow him to interact and absorb its lessons?

If you've followed what I've been saying, you know that your primary parental role, day in and day out, is to facilitate your child's play. The go-faster, workaday world in which *you* live will not work well for your children. (Don't confuse the

34

speed at which your children move when they're excited with hurrying!) They will not learn effectively and enjoy life in your fast lane.

As chief overseer of all programs, services, and products your children come into contact with, you'll need to evaluate using the following measuring stick. If you're assessing three different dancing schools, ask yourself this: *Which one of the programs will allow enough time for my child to work freely on his lessons at his own pace, with modest supervision?*

■ When Observing Other Children in a Program, Ask Yourself:

✦ Which program generates the most laughter, absorption, and enjoyment on the faces of the children?

✦ Which program focuses on personal rewards rather than technical perfection?

✦ Which program challenges and inspires the children to succeed, rather than insisting on progress?

✦ Which program has an instructor who works with all the varied talents that the pupils bring to the table, instead of placing all of the children in the same cookie cutter mold?

Don't confuse an apparently slower pace of engagement with boredom, which is something to be avoided at all costs. Boredom frequently arises when your children have no choice in what they're engaged in or no understanding of what they're doing, when they're forced to prolong the activity in spite of this, or when they're moved too quickly from one activity to the next.

CHAPTER TWO

■ Be Careful of Your Own Misguided Expectations

One place where you're likely to witness your expectations getting out of hand is in this choosing of programs, services, and products for your children. What comes to mind when you think of providing these things for your children, and whose choices are these: yours, your children's, or someone else's?

Your children's decisions are the ones most likely to prove successful, although it isn't always easy to distinguish their real preferences from those that they have been "sold"—for example, by clever TV commercials.

■ Simple Choices Are Often Best

Simple products will often satisfy your child enormously. A basic cardboard box can be far more engaging to a boy than an elaborate toy, because the box enables him to fantasize in many ways. The secret is that simple things are not so simple from a play point of view. A box can be a house, a fort, a boat, or a city, whereas an elaborate toy train can be little else but a toy train. The train itself suggests activities, whereas with the box the child's brain creates its own scenarios.

Such classic play items from nature as sand, mud, and sticks are like the box, in that they can be shaped into as many things as the child can imagine, whereas a TV program can be little but the acting out of an elaborate script. By leaning toward experiences for your child that have this open-ended, freethinking quality for her to connect with, you're facilitating the effectiveness of your child's play.

Free time is best for play; structured time, although sometimes necessary, should be kept to a minimum. Also, learning by doing is nearly always the most effective way to

36

THE PROBLEM WITH PRECONCEPTIONS

learn. It engages more of the senses, and enables a child to harmonize many things together.

Programs and services should follow the same rule of thumb. Be wary of highly structured systems that leave little or no room for variety. Your child must be empowered to use his imagination and to select his own direction, style, timing, and pacing.

A SUMMARY OF CHAPTER TWO

It's critically important that you be aware of your preconceptions about parenting before you embark on this journey, because parenting begins where your preconceptions leave off. While you're at it, you need to examine your preconceptions in general, because sooner or later they will all be reflected in your children's eyes.

The most effective parenting is achieved indirectly. This is accomplished when your children observe your everyday behavior and pattern their behavior, choices, and preferences after yours. They will pattern what you *do*, not what you say.

You cannot control your children. They will decide nearly everything in a way that suits their needs. The best you can do is respect them, expose them to as many choices as you can, and facilitate their greatest need: finding the time, place, and opportunity for free play. That is to say, allow your children to explore the world at their own pace and in their own way.

Schedule their time, and select programs, services, and products that best suit your children's preferences for play. Be very careful about overprogramming, overscheduling, or overrestricting anything they're involved in.

37

CHAPTER TWO

ASSIGNMENT FOR CHAPTER TWO

Make a recording or videotape of yourself speaking with your children, in both good times and challenged times. Then play it back for analysis. Get a second opinion, and ask your mate to comment also. You may be surprised by what you learn. Pay special attention to double standards, i.e., the way you behave while instructing your children to behave in some other way. For example, how do you respond in front of your children when you're stressed? Is this in keeping with how you advise your children to behave when they are under stress?

CHAPTER 3

The Value of Play

The fundamental job of a toddler is to rule the universe.

—Lawrence Kutner

The most natural and essential talent that children possess is, without question, the ability to play. Kids master this skill without any instruction. Give a child any group of ordinary household objects, let's say for example an egg carton and a spoon, and they will invariably create a game. For children have inexhaustible stores of imagination.

PLAY IS YOUR CHILD'S MOST IMPORTANT FUNCTION

Why is play so important to children? Play, as it concerns children, is a term that generally describes active engagement in any pleasurable, enjoyable activity of the child's own free choice, to meet the child's internal needs and accomplish the child's internal goals. (My thanks to the International Association for the Child's Right to Play for this definition.)

Play is a child's way of interacting with the world. It has a systematic relationship to what is not play. In other words, it is how the world is integrated into a child's being—digested, so to speak, and fitted into place piece by piece in an unseen mental framework. Eventually, whatever has been engaged in through play will be understood in a deeper way. As Piaget told us, play integrates all of a child's sensorimotor skills,

39

CHAPTER THREE

functional skills, and symbolic skills in close coordination with many interrelated brain functions.

Play gives children the tools they need to make sense of the world. Its combination of mimicry, exploration, fantasy, and practice is completely absorbing. All of the joy and excitement of life is wrapped up in it, and it connects the child to many mental, social, and motor skills as well as helping him to assimilate the world and all its wonders.

Play is a vital part of learning, and is how intelligence develops. Over the past 100 years, researchers too numerous to mention have been classifying and categorizing the many phases of play and child development, and exposing the important hidden linkages between play and all the systems operating in the world at large. (A few of these researchers, whose books you'll find listed in the Bibliography, are Angier, Brosterman, Buhler, Diamond, D'Arcangelo, Freud, Healy, Hull, Jambor, Koffka, Millar, Parry and Gregory, Schlosberg, Skinner, Sprenger, and Tolman.)

PARENTS SHOULD RESPECT PLAY FAR MORE THAN THEY DO
Parents needn't know everything that the researchers know, but they certainly need to understand how important play is before they disrupt play behavior or attempt to restrict it. Children need time, space, and freedom to engage in play. If they're too restricted, they may pay a high price in later life: lost mental capacity, emotional difficulties, and any number of other unforeseen problems can result. When it comes to play, children can never get enough of it, and I would argue that their quality of life depends on it.

Unfortunately, many parents are unaware of just how crucial play is. These misguided folks run their homes as what

40

THE VALUE OF PLAY

I shall call "parentocracies," which revolve around the needs and convenience of themselves rather than their children. Similarly, "teachertocracies" govern the way classrooms are run.

Expanding this even further, we might say that children are ultimately governed by "culturetocracies": religious beliefs and social norms imposed by the individual societies in which they're brought up. For example, many religions teach that the way to salvation is through work and not play. The error in these approaches is that they frequently favor teaching and learning models that suit the adults best, rather than models that favor children. American homes have become parentocracies as the result of social transformations; the extended nuclear family model of yesterday has morphed into the single-parent family of today. Apparently, as familial responsibility for children has narrowed to fewer and fewer people, the need for these forms of control has grown.

INSTITUTIONS HAVE MISGUIDED POLICIES ABOUT PLAY

Institutions such as schools and churches can thus be significant obstacles to the kind of child's play that's known to be most beneficial. Several school districts in the United States have gone so far as to take major steps to eliminate recess. Some have actually done away with it altogether!

What possible reasons could California, Florida, Georgia, Virginia, and a number of other states have given for this misguided practice? They cite falling test scores in reading and math and claim they're attempting to increase productivity, or they complain that they're being forced to manage more children with fewer teachers. This is shortsighted madness, akin to defying gravity for efficiency's sake.

CHAPTER THREE

Here's a tip: If you want to manage your child's upbringing masterfully, figure out how to make play the center of her life. One brave young housewife named Rebecca Lamphiere recently did this in Virginia Beach, Virginia. She single-handedly reversed this misguided policy and had recess put back where it belongs. For more information about Rebecca's efforts, contact her through the www.ipausa.org Web site. Rebecca has started a national organization called People CARE (People Concerned About Recess in Education).

PARENTS NEED TO BE REMINDED ABOUT THE VALUE OF PLAY

Many adults have forgotten how to play or have lowered play's priority to such a point that it occupies only a very small place in their lives. Play advocates have recognized this behavior, and have begun incorporating parental play training in their community service programs, to increase parental sensitivity and respect for play (Ashley, 2001). Who would have thought that people who have so recently emerged from childhood themselves would have to be sold on the value and benefits of movement and of having a good time? Apparently it's not self-evident that the activity and joy of play is what makes life worth living.

A SUMMARY OF CHAPTER THREE

Play is as fundamental to the essential survival of children as air. Children come into the world with all the skills they need to play, so they jump right in and explode with laughter. Very little in the way of resources is required for play. Put any humble object in a child's hands and imagination will do the rest.

Play (mimicry, exploration, fantasy, and practice) is the

42

THE VALUE OF PLAY

technique by which children assimilate, integrate, and make sense of all the world's elements, customs, and resources. All of the child's sensorimotor, functional, and symbolic skills are put to work, in coordination with all the interrelated brain, motor, and social functions. Play absorbs the child's entire attention. And it is clear from the simple observation of children's faces and voices that play is also very enjoyable. A key element of play is the requirement that it be of a child's free choice, to meet that child's own internal needs and goals.

As clear as is the value and importance of play to all children, it remains a mystery why so many parents, teachers, and social institutions (such as churches, community groups, government agencies, and nonprofit organizations) prioritize play so far down the list when it comes to family, school, and social organizations. Instead of respecting the needs of children for play, parents, teachers, and administrators manage their homes, schools, and institutions around their own adult needs and time schedules—as parentocracies, teachertocracies, and culturetocracies. This specifically means that play is defined, confined, and restricted whenever it conflicts with home, school, church, community, or government operations. In effect, play is being culturally negated by these other requirements.

In a child's life, overrestricting play probably has negative consequences of lifelong duration. Adults who have forgotten the importance of the joy of play probably have trouble coming up with valid reasons for living. Those without clear reasons for living cannot be leading very fulfilling lives, because they're not meeting their own needs. Parents who understand this will understand that play needs to be put back into the center of their children's lives.

CHAPTER THREE

ASSIGNMENT FOR CHAPTER THREE

Picture, then list on the left side of a piece of notepaper, a few goings-on that you can still remember having as a child—activities that you did in your free time anywhere, then that you did in your home with your family, then that you did in school, then that you did in your church. Picture anything that comes to mind, pleasant or unpleasant.

Next, again list on the left side of a piece of notepaper a few memorable activities that you did within the past year. Once again, picture anything that comes to mind, pleasant or unpleasant. Make sure you say where each of these occurred (at home, at work, or elsewhere).

In the right column, score each activity from 1 to 10, with 10 being the most enjoyable and 1 being the least enjoyable of all the items listed.

Now answer these questions related to this list:

✦ What can you say about the rules and restrictions placed on those items on the list?

✦ Do the items with the highest, most favorable rankings correspond to greater or fewer restrictions?

Now answer these general questions:

✦ As a child in school, which did you enjoy more: your time at recess or the time you spent in class?

✦ As a child with your parents, which did you enjoy more: time spent on a family outing or time spent engaged in your own activities?

✦ As a child at home, which did you enjoy more: playing in your own back yard with facilities provided by your

44

THE VALUE OF PLAY

parents or playing in your neighborhood community in places of your own choosing?

✦ In which places did you most enjoy playing? Did these places have more or less overt restrictions placed on them, compared to other places you might have chosen?

CHAPTER 4

Planning for Your Children's Lives

I will always cherish the initial misconceptions I had . . .

– Unknown

Some animals are self-sufficient from the moment of birth. They literally hit the ground running, and don't need a parent's help. You have probably witnessed this phenomenon on television: aquatic and insect embryos being left by their mothers to fend for themselves without so much as a hello. Scores of the tiny creatures do not survive, but the sheer numbers guarantee that the species will go on. Compared to larger animals and humans, their life spans are short and their survival skills limited (although apparently sufficient to have sustained them for millennia).

Furthermore, it's a fact that some mammals are born with innate, fairly complex skills. Deer, for example, are able to stand upright moments after being born, and begin walking shortly thereafter. Many species do spend time teaching their young essential skills such as self-defense, territory marking, and food gathering, but most animals don't come close to spending the years that humans do in bringing up their offspring.

WE TAKE OUR TIME RAISING OUR YOUNG

Human parents have chosen not to follow the hands-off strategy that other species have adopted. Scientists say that we'd be unable to follow it with any success, anyway. We have an instrument that might make survival possible without much assistance: our brain. But few human children could successfully handle all the challenges inherent in daily life without a significant amount of support from adults.

Most human parents expect their offspring to enjoy a long and prosperous life and to employ a wide variety of skills for survival, fulfillment, and enjoyment. In order to ensure these desired outcomes, parents in westernized civilizations have adapted to highly prolonged child-rearing periods, some of the longest of any species. Having one's young at home for 18 to 22 years is not at all unusual, though this amounts to 20–25 percent or more of an average life span. Some parents devote an even longer time to the raising of their children.

WHY REINVENT THE WHEEL?

Lengthy as these time frames may be, childcare experts regard them as necessary for the benefit of children and society, and as significant time and resource savers when compared to learning by trial and error or other methods. Perhaps this is just common sense: why should it be necessary to reinvent the wheel time and again? It is much more efficient to pass on information about the wheel to our offspring through education. After all, successful living is a complex enterprise. It takes a significant amount of preparation and practice to master all the necessary skills. We have so much to learn in so little time.

CHAPTER FOUR

Are we correct in choosing to parent for so long? I say yes. It is technically possible, but generally unfeasible and highly unlikely, that a child would successfully survive, be fulfilled, or achieve significant enjoyment in life without extended and persistent parenting. From time to time, I do hear about a case where the odds seem to have been beaten. When I investigate, however, it's more than likely a case of substitution by different methods of parenting, or parenting by unconventional methods, rather than a lack of any parenting at all.

IF EXTENSIVE PARENTING IS COMMON SENSE, WHY DO SOME PARENTS FALL SHORT?

The idea that children need a long period of parenting is widely accepted. Why, then, do a significant number of parents defy the odds regarding their children's future and fail to parent long enough, or parent ineffectively? What are some of the factors that cause certain parents to abbreviate the time they spend raising their kids?

■ Real-World Economics

Some parents have been forced to curtail their child-rearing efforts by economic constraints. This is a reasonable explanation in light of the amount of economic hardship in the world. Globally, most people need to work daily to survive, and many parents have to work two jobs to make ends meet. Many children have single parents—a circumstance that also significantly restricts parenting time. Further, a U.S. Dept. of Agriculture study has shown that families increase their educational spending in direct proportion to their incomes (Lino, 1999).

48

PLANNING FOR YOUR CHILDREN'S LIVES

■ Social Class

Children of differing social classes are not brought up in the same ways, and it's not simply a matter of economics. For one thing, different social classes place varying degrees of emphasis on the educational value of the activities they choose for their children.

■ Culture

Cultures differ significantly in the priority they place upon education vs. other activities. I'm speaking of culture in a broad sense—differences between men and women (who may be involved in single parenting); differences between immigrant parents and third-generation parents (in the U.S.A.); and differences between parents involved in orthodox religions and those who are less religiously engaged.

■ Beliefs

For a variety of reasons, parents differ in their beliefs about the amount of nurturing, which they may see as coddling, that is necessary for their children to thrive.

■ Ignorance

Some parents are simply not aware of the relationship between childhood nurturing and life success.

■ A Lack of Training in Parenting

Another reason may be that some individuals have never learned the skills necessary to be parents. Therefore they have, among other things, an insufficient appreciation of the necessity for good parenting. Perhaps they believe that

49

CHAPTER FOUR

growing up is a function that works best on automatic pilot, requiring minimal assistance. It may be that many people fall into this untrained category, for parenting is not an educational course commonly taught in school.

In the past, we've depended upon our parents and families to teach us about parenting. With extended families no longer performing the parental training functions they once did, child-rearing success may be moving in the direction of, say, a fish surviving its parent's abandonment shortly after spawning.

Lack of education in parenting may lead to a number of related beliefs and expectations. For instance, parents don't believe in what to them seems like excessive mentoring. Such parents may have placed unrealistically high expectations upon substitute parenting; they may believe that their children will fulfill their own developmental needs without mentoring assistance, or may believe that their children are in the capable-enough category and don't require assistance.

■ A Lack of Skills

There may be other reasons that some parents don't parent adequately, beside a lack of general parental training. The parenting skills required in different circumstances vary considerably. They are affected by a large number of factors, not the least of which is the difference in the character and personality of the children under care. I believe that each child is very different—so much so that the skills adequate to parent one child may not be sufficient for another. This can certainly be the case in a given family, where parents find one child easy to work with and another quite the opposite!

50

PLANNING FOR YOUR CHILDREN'S LIVES

■ Communication Issues

Another reason may be that certain parents have considerable communication difficulties or other sorts of problems with their children. These can result in discouragement for the parents as well as a lack of confidence in their own efforts, and it follows that their children may not respect their efforts.

Communication difficulties can be related to other problems that I have addressed in this book. For example, parents may lack understanding about the most effective methods of influencing their children. The inability to connect with their kids may be an offshoot of never learning how to parent in general, or parent a certain kind of child in particular. A lack of communication skills may be the primary parental deficiency.

■ Family Structure

Many alternative family structures exist in today's world. Children are being raised by peers, siblings, in-laws, nonrelatives, stepparents, institutions, and in other nontraditional arrangements. Under such circumstances, a given family structure may not be conducive to a particular child's needs.

■ Other Issues

There may also be other problems. Many of us have had the experience of not getting along with someone. In the case of families, some individuals may not like their own children, or may like only some of them. Unfortunate though it may be, some parents may not like children, period . . . anyone's children.

CHAPTER FOUR

■ Other Priorities

Finally, some parents can't or may not want to take the time necessary to engage in good parenting, because they prefer to spend their time in other pursuits. This may be temporary or may be more permanent. In the least fortunate case, certain parents may not like parenting compared to their other obligations, and may not fully embrace their parental duties. They may not have time for the kind of committed effort that bringing up children requires. Perhaps they are fundamentally self-centered or withdrawn. Spending time elsewhere on other pursuits may be either a necessity or simply a matter of preference.

SOME SAVING GRACES

Thank goodness we don't get born into the world completely unprepared. We get a lot of help from our genetic background, as well as from everyone and everything we contact.

■ Genetics

Our genes predispose us to many important talents. The musical prodigies among us can begin singing world-class arias from the first time they hear an opera, for example. Others can do advanced math, chemistry, and physics seemingly without effort—activities most would find quite difficult. Still others are "born to lead," "born to sell," or "born to invent."

The majority of us aren't so fortunate as to have extraordinary skills, however, and have only average inclinations . . . maybe even below-average inclinations. The list of basic skills with which we are equipped from birth is extensive, and only partially known to science. We can name examples

52

PLANNING FOR YOUR CHILDREN'S LIVES

that are obvious to any observer of young babies, including basic sensory skills, motor control, and mimicry. By extraordinary skills, I mean those that appear to come out of nowhere — that is, from no obvious influence. Almost any keen observer of small children can cite examples that defy explanation.

■ Development

Development means the taking of our genetic raw material and intentionally nurturing it, shaping it, and coaxing it into its final form. This takes effort, consistency, and practice. Throughout our childhoods, we are works in progress. Some of our development we initiate ourselves, using basic skills we're born with or those taught to us. Development also comes directly from good nutrition, and from the tutelage and influence of our parents. Still other development comes from the outside world of friends, relatives, teachers, acquaintances, and mentors, as well the various media available to most westernized people, such as books, newspapers, magazines, movies, and television.

■ A Child's Calling

Nature and nurture will make way for something else within the child: a calling. Children are born with some of the traits of their ancestors. They also have different developmental experiences that set them apart. But a third major influence comes from the depths of the child herself. It is a unique character and calling that distinguishes that child from all other children and indeed all other humans — "a soul's code," if you will (Hillman, 1996).

A calling is a motivating force within a child that directs

53

her choices and activities toward an end that suits her. It is accessible to no one else, and beyond the reach of her parents and peers. It speaks to the child and the child alone.

Parenting has little influence here, in that a child's calling will persist regardless. If parents are perceptive enough to recognize their child's calling, they can support and enhance it, but they cannot stifle or extinguish it for long.

■ We Learn Some Things by Ourselves

A child develops and learns by any number of means beside the experience of being parented. Depending on their age, the following are some of the means that children use to develop themselves *by* themselves: observation, listening, exploration, trial and error, practice, playing, fantasizing, and independent invention.

■ Other Things We Learn from Others

Skills we learn from others include all forms of interactive communication, including speech, language, writing, reading, drawing, role-playing, and group game playing.

This interactive learning doesn't happen in a vacuum, however. The context of all our early learning is provided by our parents, from the type of home environment they create to the psychological culture of love, patience, and steady support that, optimally, they surround us with.

HOME BASE

Throughout the upbringing process, our home is our base. Home is the nursery of our upbringing, including the bed we lie in, the people with whom we spend the most time, the walls within which we live, and finally the neighborhood that surrounds us, including the community, state, and nation. Our home, in this broad sense, must provide almost all the resources necessary for our development and the enrichment of our body, mind, and spirit.

Having a reasonably stable home provides a base of familiarity that grows over time, enabling a child to devote energy to other activities that need attending to.

■ The Home Culture

A development-friendly atmosphere in the home environment makes an enormous difference in childhood development. By development-friendly atmosphere, I mean a safe, non-threatening, minimally disturbing place where childhood learning can take place without undue interference from hazards, distractions, and annoyances. Children must have space, time, and freedom to develop. If they must fight with siblings, contend with significant restrictions, or put up with noise or other environmental influences that hinder concentration, then character building and development will not proceed efficiently. Hence, providing and maintaining a nurturing environment is clearly a parental responsibility of the first order.

■ Parental Input

A child's development will continue without parental support, but probably not very well. At the very least, support begins by providing a home and helpful home culture that stands ready to assist the developing child. At best, good parenting input includes a devoted, nurturing attitude, one-on-one guidance, and personal participation keyed to the individual needs of the particular child.

CHAPTER FOUR

DEVELOPMENTAL DIFFERENCES

Although many of us believe that most Americans live in comparable circumstances, there are considerable differences in the development of different individuals, stemming from the inputs that contribute to their maturity. We see and hear all the time about children who have deprived, average, and privileged upbringings. We witness the differing outcomes for these children. While there is no perfectly predictable causal linkage between the quality of a childhood and its outcome, I feel confident in making a few simple propositions.

■ Childhood Stimuli Enhance Success

The more childhood development inputs we receive, the more our chances for a successful life are increased. As children, working with the right tools increases our personal, physical, and cognitive productivity. We spin our wheels less. We live longer lives, appreciate life more, and are more fulfilled. By more development inputs, I mean more stimuli in childhood and more learning over time.

Solid scientific findings back this up. In the past ten years, brain researchers have discovered that increased early childhood stimulus generates the growth of more nerve endings in the brain — dendrites that are critical in development (Diamond, 1998). This contradicts what many of us may have been taught: that we lose brain cells every day, implying that we become less capable the older and more experienced we get. Apparently nothing could be further from the truth. Diamond and many other researchers have shown that what will make us lose brain cells (besides drug abuse) is a lack of stimuli.

56

PLANNING FOR YOUR CHILDREN'S LIVES

■ First, the Basics

Children can't be broadly enriched until they are first narrowly enriched. Granted, enrichment in a wide variety of skills is an ultimate goal in personal development, but this enrichment must start small. That is to say, it must proceed step by step, with the learning of one skill at a time. When a child has mastered the basics, we can then build upon the shoulders of those fundamental skills.

If a child is starved of basic enrichment (such as, for example, a consistent course in reading), he will lack the tools he needs to progress. It is critically important for him to master the basics early, because he will face an exceptionally wide range of experiences later on, and be called upon to perform any number of tasks as an independent adult. Preparation for this takes considerable time, exposure, and practice, and any time lost through enrichment starvation can have major impacts upon his future life.

■ Learning How to Learn

One of the most important areas of childhood development is learning how to learn. A child is born with many key tools already in place, such as memory, visualization, verbalization, and logical reasoning. But along the way she needs to be given the other, equally important tools described above. The earlier we employ strategies to allow our children to use and enhance their genetic gifts, the better. More effective learning methods lead to more efficient development.

Every individual has different learning preferences. Clearly, we need to discover what these are early on. Learning styles are neither equal in importance nor equal in their

57

CHAPTER FOUR

ease of attainment for each child. For example, some children learn by visualizing far more effectively than they do by hearing a verbal description.

On the subject of learning preferences, play is proving to be the most important learning tool in early childhood, especially for children of elementary school age and below. Child-centered play, according to the International Association for the Child's Right to Play, is freely chosen by the child to meet needs chosen by the child and directed toward fulfilling the goals of the child. Adult-imposed play is different. In child-directed play, children develop important self-management skills through fantasy, mimicry, and role-playing. They learn to regulate the flow of stimuli coming their way—a skill that's important in preparing their brains for academic learning in their later years (Ashley, 2001).

Sufficient space, time, and materials, as well as a nurturing attitude, are of fundamental importance to this learning. Unstructured, unhurried, and parentally supported free time for play is critical, especially in the early years. Parents need to trust their children's instincts and give their youngsters the freedom to thoroughly explore their play surroundings. With repeated activities of children's own choosing, familiarity and a sense of safety set in, followed by exploration and inquiry. Children need this entire context to absorb the lesson that their play is intrinsically valuable.

Playtime should not be granted as a reward for good behavior, nor restricted as punishment for undesired behavior. To children, play is as important as breathing. No one would even consider restricting breathing as a prerequisite to living; and so it should be with play. Play is much too important to be used by adults to control a child's behavior. With successful,

58

unimpeded play comes children's ability to become thriving, independent adults, through mastering a set of learning processes that will serve them for the rest of their lives.

The home is probably the most effective setting for early childhood education, given that the home setting is highly conducive to learning. A safe and secure home setting will enable a child to keep going beyond the learning levels that have already been attained.

DEVELOPMENT IS EXPENSIVE, BUT NO ONE CAN AFFORD TO GO WITHOUT IT

If you think education is expensive, try ignorance.

– Derek Bok

Development is arguably the most expensive commonplace undertaking in which humans engage. It takes an enormous amount of time, energy, support, care, practice, and patience. Development is expensive in every conceivable way. It is possible, but highly undesirable, to shortcut the developmental process. Could we survive on only half the amount of water, oxygen, food, and love that we're accustomed to receiving? Perhaps. But why on earth would we want to? It's the same with learning. Development is a basic building block of life whose importance can't be overestimated.

THE CHARACTERISTICS OF GOOD PARENTING

A sense of worthiness is a child's most important need.

– Polly Berrien Berends

Good parenting, as I define it, is behavior that provides the best possible environment for the upbringing of children.

CHAPTER FOUR

The following are some of the most important characteristics of good parenting.

■ Unconditional Emotional Support

First and foremost, good parenting provides unconditional emotional support. Children need to know that they are standing upon a solid foundation that is absolutely helpful, compassionate, encouraging, caring, and loyal in all situations, so that they can do what they need to do (develop) with emotional freedom. This development must take place in an environment free from the fear of reprisals, ridicule, physical abuse, hidden penalties, or hurtful consequences. For example, when a child makes a mistake or does something wrong, a good parent tries to look beyond the moment to the essence of the behavior and give gentle, constructive guidance that will result in a more successful behavior the next time the child encounters a similar situation.

■ Courage, Dedication, and Concentration

Growing up successfully means making major physical, mental, and emotional leaps forward. The process is demanding. It can be frustrating, difficult, and disappointing at times, despite good parental guidance. That's why courage, dedication, and concentration on the parents' part are additional traits needed to help get children through it.

■ Trustworthiness

In learning to walk, children must fall down, scrape their knees, perhaps conk their heads, cry, get up, and try again many times to get it right. The last thing they need while all of this is going on is to have their emotional support pulled

60

out from under them by their parents. What I'm talking about here is the need for trustworthiness. Parents must be trustworthy so that they can earn their children's trust. What is trustworthiness to a child? It means being reliable, supportive, and comforting—walking one's talk.

WHAT KIND OF PARENTING MAKES CHILDREN MOST COMFORTABLE?

To children childhood holds no particular advantage.

– Kathleen Norris

The supervision given to children, while absolutely necessary and undeniably helpful in the long run, is not always pleasant to the child being guided or to those around that child as the guidance is occurring. Parents who micromanage their children also make them highly uncomfortable. Who among us grownups would enjoy being directly accountable to someone for everything we do twenty-four hours of every day, for a period of at least eighteen years? Does the concept of imprisonment come to mind?

■ Forming a Working Relationship

While there is no magical method of parenting that will appeal to all children, we do want our children to be as receptive as possible to what we have to offer them. What we're talking about here is the need for a working relationship—one that can be counted upon on a daily basis to get you and your child through most situations with your feelings intact. I'm speaking about a general approach to parenting, and by this I mean any number of policies, rules, strategies, plans, guiding principles, courses of action, procedures, and philosophies

CHAPTER FOUR

that are effective in working with your children and getting
the family through each day. I'm not addressing biological
parents only; this advice is for all who take on the role of
parent.

For example, what do you do when your child does
something really dangerous? What if she climbs up on your
steeply pitched roof and runs around? Can you think of any
responses to this situation that will endear you to your child?
I can't. What I *can* envision is putting a stop to the behavior
as quickly as possible. What do you do when your teenaged
son shrugs and says "No problem" when asked if he will
make an increased effort to raise his grade point average a
notch above "F"? If you're stumped, you might try reading
Bill Cosby's best-selling book, *Fatherhood*. What do you do
when your daughter, in a playful, rambunctious moment,
destroys your priceless heirloom glassware, and in the process sustains a serious injury? As a parent, I'd be working very
hard to restrain my emotions in this case.

■ Making the Best of a Love-Hate Situation

In parent-child situations, we have to make the best of a
love-hate situation — a classic dilemma. Children simultaneously love their parents and hate being parented. They
want advice, yet often resent it. They crave hearing what you
have to say, but after hearing you, they'll act as they please.
It's an irony surrounded by an enigma wrapped in a paradox.
Although I had a very happy childhood, when I became a
teenager I remember often wondering how long I had to
go before I'd be free, free, free! Forming a good working
relationship with your child will help smooth the rocky road
of parenting.

62

PLANNING FOR YOUR CHILDREN'S LIVES

A FEW TIME-PROVEN PARENTING POLICIES

It's tricky to generalize about a given parenting approach, because all children and all parents have different temperaments and parenting involves an interaction between parents and children that is complex and ever-changing. Having said that, I still want to offer a few general parenting policies that, when put into action, have stood the test of time.

■ Bowing to Individual Temperament

Matching your parenting approach to each child's individual temperament is highly important. By paying attention to your children, you'll discover after some experimentation what works and what flops with each one.

Some extensive reading of research and my own personal experience have taught me that children are born with distinctive personality traits. Some kids are full of excitement and nervous energy. Others are stubborn. Still others are quiet and reflective. These traits may not be consistent; some are part of a personality "repertoire" that your children draw from in working with you — temporary and periodic moods that pass through their beings.

■ Matching Each Unique Personality with a Unique Parenting Approach

Working with each one of your children's characteristic personality stances requires a different parenting approach. With the excited child, humor might work well as a parental personality match, yet humor might fall flat for the reflective child. Meanwhile, some serious bribery might work like a charm with the stubborn one. One child responds favorably to challenges and dares in a wide range of situations. Another

63

CHAPTER FOUR

one jumps at invitations and other distractions. Still another wants no part of cooperative interaction, preferring that a parent just watch and keep a distance. There is no single right answer here, except to find an approach for each child that matches well enough so that he or she responds favorably to you—that part is important.

In conjunction with this, one very crucial question needs to be asked: Do you need to suspend your own personality or temperament to do this successfully? Yes, you do. How good will you be at doing this? Well, how flexible are you?

■ Giving Your Undivided Attention

Paying undivided attention to children is incredibly important. Children don't want to be told what to do; they want to be given approval for what they do. By paying attention, I mean full, undivided "eyes on" and "hands on" attention. Further, I mean no talking with friends on the phone while standing by, no head in the newspaper, no glazed eyes, and no wandering mind. You know what I'm talking about. You don't like it when someone does this to you when *you're* trying to communicate. It conveys a lack of respect, you grumble to yourself. Guess what! Your kids don't like it either. They feel disrespected, despite your best efforts to keep your wandering attention from being obvious. Trust me that your child needs your full attention. On your side, if you have your attention focused on your child's performance or conversation, good ideas will start flowing into your mind about what you can do to help your child grow up more enriched and capable. You'll enjoy the interaction more and get more out of it.

Naturally, paying full attention is not always easy to do for a busy, responsible parent. This is one of the most difficult

PLANNING FOR YOUR CHILDREN'S LIVES

challenges for me, for I can't just switch off my brain to all the important things I must do on a daily basis. I'm sure you feel the same way. But you must resist this feeling and concentrate on your child when you're with him or her. Try to make this a standard you live up to. If you're going to give your progeny some of your all-too-scarce time, then either give the child your 100 percent-focused attention or don't give any time at all until you can give it in this way.

■ **First Observe, Then Acknowledge, and Finally Judge**
Here is a piece of wisdom for parents to use in dealing with their children: Pay careful attention first, *then* take action, if any is needed at all. You might try memorizing this statement if you're having problems in this area: *I will count slowly to fifty before acting on any first impulse with my children.* Parental regard is an important confirmation that those emotional parental "legs" are solidly present. Observation doesn't have to mean agreement or approval; simple acknowledgment is the key. You need to observe and then acknowledge what's going on, before considering judgment. While children crave affirmation, they may cringe in the face of accountability. Double-check your face for any judgmental attitude you may be wearing for them.

■ **Showing Up Is at Least 90 Percent of Good Parenting**
Being physically present with your children and emotionally accessible to them is all-important. Your youngsters won't understand your excuses and rationalizations, although they have no trouble with their own. From a child's perspective, either a parent is there when he is needed or he is not. There's little to no gray area here—no middle ground for

65

CHAPTER FOUR

equivocation. Children don't like being answerable to someone twenty-four hours a day, but they do need a continual
stream of affirmations and praise. And here's another piece
of friendly advice: When in doubt, *show up*. Who was it who
said that showing up is 90 percent of being successful? There
is wisdom in this as it applies to successful parenting. Soccer
moms know this. You don't need to fawn all over them. Just
showing up might be enough to serve as an affirmation.
(And giving your undivided attention after you show up
could have the kids nominating you for parent of the year!)

■ Judgment Is the Ultimate Hot Potato

No one can help being judgmental. It's a necessary survival
tactic that we all employ. After all, going through life successfully means making good choices. Making choices means
making assessments, appraisals, evaluations, reviews, considerations, and measurements . . . in short, many judgments.
But communicating your judgments about your children's
behavior must be handled delicately and with careful focus,
lest you injure them or be seriously maimed yourself.

Children want their parents to behave like dogs; that is to
say, to be there for them reliably no matter what, with happy
wagging tails, sloppy kisses, and big grins. You got it—children
want unconditional love, not judgments. Unfortunately,
good parenting gets in the way of that. You, as parent, need
to judge your children's behavior constantly because that's
your role and responsibility. You love them, you're looking
after them, and you want no harm to come to them. You
also realize that children have inadequate experience for
making good decisions. What other choice do you have but
to be a big bad judge?

66

PLANNING FOR YOUR CHILDREN'S LIVES

Here's the trick: the problem is not in being judgmental. It's in the style and timing of your delivery. By style, I mean the tone of your voice, the rapidity of your speech, and the intensity of your facial expressions.

I'm not asking that you confuse or patronize your children by delivering mixed messages, i.e., saying critical things in a nice way. By all means, be as truthful as you can. But do so without being hurtful. I am asking that you carefully consider your presentation as part of your overall approach. This entire issue is so important that I've broken it down into six parts.

How to Make Judgments (When You Must)

1. *Consider the long-term impact of your message.*
The most important issue in presenting your judgment to your children is *not* the specific judgment you wish to communicate about a specific act. Rather, what is most important is to teach your children how to make judgments by themselves about their own choices and those of others.

In my own parenting, my goal was always to start a mental process in my child so that, whenever she was faced with a choice, her brain followed the very procedures I used to judge her choices. My thinking was that if I did this in a fair and reasonable manner, she would feel compelled to follow my lead in the future. For example, if she brought home a good report card with the exception of one or two less-than-stellar performances, I would follow a standard procedure that began with a series of questions something like this: How did you do this past quarter? What was your favorite class? What was your least favorite class? What subject did you learn the most from? What was the most interesting thing you learned? Did

67

CHAPTER FOUR

you have any problems? What could you have done better? Did you deserve the grades you got?

Of course I didn't ask her *all* of these questions, nor did I fire off my questions in rapid order. We engaged in a friendly exchange, including all those pleasantries that accompany the best conversations. I would ask her a question, then listen to her response. I might ask her for clarification of a point or two. Then I would take it in and gradually and comfortably ask another question, taking my personality out of the equation and shifting the focus to the stories she told. Depending upon the specific answers to her questions, I would then share similar experiences that I had had, so that she would know that I had empathy for the situations she faced. I wouldn't go overboard in giving her information. Instead, I would say something like, "You know, I had that happen to me several times." I would tell her some of the specifics, but would not tell her how the situation got resolved, or the lessons I learned, or any advice I might have to give her about her situation. Instead, I would wait until she decided to ask me for more details.

She would ask me about some of my experiences right away. On others, I would get a question out of the blue a few days, weeks, or months later. Whenever the questions came, I would give out as little information as possible until she pushed me. When she got to the point of asking me what I had learned from an experience, my judgment of her situation would be embedded in how I resolved my own situation. In this way, I was able to avoid rushing to judgment and retain my credibility in dispensing advice to a daughter who was willing to listen because she was seeking alternative solutions. Most importantly, she was able to proceed to do as I did (and possibly improve upon it) instead of just doing as I said

68

PLANNING FOR YOUR CHILDREN'S LIVES

(which she probably would have ignored or at least not have taken as seriously).

2. Assemble the facts.

I strongly advise that you never proceed with an evaluation of your children's behavior or performance until you know all the facts, or as many of them as you can piece together within a reasonable time frame. Please carefully consider this advice. It is crucial. Additionally, don't assume that your children will present you with all of the facts. They may not know all the facts, remember all of them, or even want to disclose or discuss all of them. You may have to dig, and if you're going to dig, do so gently and with great care.

You don't want to get into the habit of rushing to judgment without the facts. This behavior will be part of your long-term impact upon your children. If you don't want them to rush to the judgment of others, then don't do this yourself. I always have to remind myself to be humble in this matter. I am by nature impatient and have, as a parent, a tendency to consider myself omniscient. By now, I have learned many times over that I am not the world's expert at getting all the facts I need by the time I have to make a judgment. Don't repeat my mistakes if you can help it.

3. Clarify your intentions.

One of my cats personifies the term "scaredy cat." She is so afraid of anything and everything that she assumes every move I make will result in her downfall. Consequently, when I move in her direction or get too close, she scampers away at top speed. When she does gather up the rare courage to come close to me, she backs toward me, presumably so she can be

CHAPTER FOUR

ready to run away quickly if I try any funny business. I have never given her any reason to act this way. I have never raised a hand to her. I pet her gently. I feed her reliably and try in every way to make her life comfortable, safe, and secure. I can't speak cat, nor can she speak human, so we are limited to actions rather than speech (although she does talk a lot for a cat, and I respond in cat-like tones to her comments). The point of the story is that I can never clarify my intentions with her, so she assumes the worst—presumably that I'm going to make her into cat stew. I see the situation as nearly hopeless; this cat will never trust me.

I hope that you will never have a child like this cat. Thankfully, trust is something that can be earned by most human parents even when their children are too young to understand their human talk. When children are old enough, they should be told what your expectations are for their behavior so that they are at all times clear. Nothing destroys trust and confidence more than being blindsided by tacit expectations. It is much easier and more pleasant to state an expectation to a child at the outset. If you ever do catch yourself being unclear—for example, being disappointed in your child's behavior when you never prepared her with your expectations—just keep it to yourself. Don't burden your child with your issue. It would be totally unfair of you.

Clarifying your intentions is a huge part of making judgments. There is no getting around having to make judgments as a parent, so making your intentions clear as early as possible makes judging as comfortable as it can ever get.

4. *Remove as many unnecessary influences as possible.*
From time to time, with no apparent warning, all hell can

70

PLANNING FOR YOUR CHILDREN'S LIVES

break loose. Yes, life is sometimes stressful, hectic and out of control—pushing you to a breaking point. At such times, it is the height of folly to do anything important with your children such as settling difficulties, differences, and misunderstandings. You are probably at your weakest at such times. It's best to call a time out and wait for a calmer period and cooler emotions. I'm sure you also know that it's much easier to do than undo. Doing what you don't intend, then denying that you intended it, delivers a very mixed message that you don't want to be associated with, especially if it occurs again and again. When in doubt, don't go ahead with decisions having to do with your children. Avoid these until the storms have passed you by. Remember that in dealing with children, you are probably engaged with skin thinner than yours, i.e., more sensitive to criticism. Keep your perspective about you. Keep smiling if you can. Be cheerful. Make sure no one but your child hears you when you speak your judgments. Speak softly and slowly if you can. All of this is harder than it appears, so you may need to practice your approach to get better. It is neither necessary nor even desirable for your children to see all the pressures that you are under. All they expect is that you be fair and consistent with them. They can be erratic, but they won't understand it when they see you being that way. You should do your best to keep your adult world to yourself or at least keep it away from your children until they are ready to merge into it with their training wheels on.

5.   *Consider the timing of your pronouncements.*

Related to the previous point, we can say with certainty that the timing of judgments is very important. There is a time for judgment and a time for letting things pass. I once knew the

CHAPTER FOUR

friend of an important mayor who would always tell me that he was the mayor's best friend because he knew, presumably through trial and error, precisely the best time to approach the mayor with problems or bad news. My friend's motto was "All issues in their own time." He would never present an issue to the mayor until the mayor's mood was right or the day seemed to be smiling and ready for the kind of news he had to deliver.

This story illustrates the importance of being equally sensitive to your children's moods. Those of us who have children all know the telltale signs of the wrong moment: the fitfulness, the crankiness. Presenting anything during a tantrum, no matter how delicate your approach, would be a disaster, as you know all too well!

6. *Match your approach to your child's mood.*
Ideally, it would be best to match your approach (for passing judgment) to your child's mood. For example, if she is really cranky, take no action; if she is just crabby, but not quite cranky, walk on eggshells if you must stand and deliver; and if she is somewhere between neutral and happy, approach things with a pleasant clarity. If you can wait for the right time, go ahead and wait. But if you can't wait, what might be best is to invent a general approach that can be used for most moods. One idea is to go for the funny bone. Try the Italian movie actor Roberto Begnini's *Life Is Beautiful* approach: humor—the more bizarre the better. Humor is a magic elixir that can accomplish miracles for those who master it.

Another approach that has worked for me is skillful questioning. I've found I can make almost all the points I want to

PLANNING FOR YOUR CHILDREN'S LIVES

by asking subtle, "soft ball" type questions rather than being demonstrative with stone tablets delivered from on high. If my daughter was being crabby, I'd just ask her firmly, persistently, and nicely a whole series of tender, loving questions. It was a technique I used that took the edge off my criticism while letting her know that I was trying my best to help her without telling her what to do.

There's also virtue in using whatever works best for you as a result of firsthand experimentation. Think of things that have made your child laugh before, and experiment to see if you can come up with a similar approach. Practice your questioning technique. Use the charm that has made you the success that you are. And once you've found the trick that works, don't let go. Run, run, run it into the ground until it won't work any more. Think of your techniques as a kind of fairy dust — a spoonful of sugar to make the medicine go down, as Mary Poppins would say.

■ Effective Coaching Isn't Easy

What I've been talking about in presenting judgments to your children is, in a larger sense, coaching. Coaching skills are valuable in parenting, for coaching children is as much about communication as anything. It is that, and a lot of other things as well. Topping the list are listening and observation — skills that are critical to communication. After trust has been established, negotiating clear and reasonable win-win agreements is also important, as is skillful refereeing. Reasoning through complex issues in language that children understand is important too.

All of this is not easy. It might be helpful to imagine

CHAPTER FOUR

yourself as a foreign diplomat in a difficult post. You must choose your methods very carefully and apply your chosen techniques in a practiced and skillful manner.

Effective coaching, contrary to some popular beliefs, is neither dictatorship nor throwing tantrums. Most coaches that get consistent results aren't like Bobby Knight, the infamous Indiana University basketball coach. They don't throw chairs around to get their way. They describe their expectations very clearly, observe performance very carefully, then give feedback in the form of rewards or effectively share helpful suggestions. Many different styles can make for effective coaching, but the underlying essentials are all very similar.

■ Work with Your Children's Motivations, Not Against Them

You can bring forth everything necessary to your children to get them interested in learning, but you can't make them apply themselves. They must take that final step by themselves.

Children seem to know quite early that they are responsible for motivating their own behavior. Parents should not try to control motivation so much as they should work *with* the motivations that come out of their children to find more effective expressions for them.

For example, you may have a boy who you think should learn about "guy stuff" like construction tools, so out of the blue you go ahead and buy him a set of play tools. You enthusiastically describe the function and purpose of these tools when you give them to him, but to your disappointment he shows little interest. What then should you do?

Well, for one thing, rethink your conclusion that he should be exposed to tools. The smarter way to act would

74

PLANNING FOR YOUR CHILDREN'S LIVES

have been in response to his strong signals that he wanted to help you when he watched you or others fixing things. The motivation would therefore have came from him, and you would simply have been giving shape to his desire. The difference between the two scenarios is enormous. Better to divert your energies to working with your children's own motivations rather than inserting or substituting your own.

WHAT SHOULD A PARENT DO TO FACILITATE DEVELOPMENT?

> *I was toilet trained at gunpoint.*
>
> – Billy Braver

Previously, I defined development as taking a child's genetic raw material and intrinsic character and gradually shaping it using all the resources parents can afford to allow for development to proceed. Parents can and should get involved with the *who*, the *what*, the *where*, and the *when* of development. Anything less is minimal development of your children, and that is a very scary concept to me. Minimal development is not a choice, and effective childhood development isn't some impossible ideal. It's an imperative.

■ Making Developmental Choices: The Essence of Parenting Today

The selection of your child's development programs, delegating these choices to the right mentors, and the managing of these mentors effectively are the key issues facing most parents today. There are very few parents who can directly provide the programs, services, and products their children need. A lot of help must come from outside the family circle,

75

CHAPTER FOUR

and will include teachers, doctors, authors, athletic coaches, clergy, computer specialists, summer program providers, advisors, and music instructors, to name just a few. Parents today "outsource" almost all of their children's needs for development programs.

In the broad view, all this delegation may be positive, for it takes some pressure off the very challenging task of effective parenting. The overall management function of parenting is difficult enough, without the complication of also being a development program provider. We live in a world of specialization today, where it is possible to find people who can do and teach nearly anything we can imagine very, very well, and usually much better than we ever could. For example, can you teach your child to become a world-class gymnast? The answer is probably not, unless you are a world-class gymnast yourself.

Of course, the delegation and management of those you have given your authority to is also a demanding skill, and I will say more about that a little later.

■ Maintaining an Overview

One good thing about delegating some of your parental authority to experts is it frees up your time and energy to focus on more important parental duties. And what are these? Well, by far the most important parental duty is providing unconditional and unwavering love and attention to your children. Everyone reading this book should be absolutely clear about this by now, so I won't dwell on it too much here. What is perhaps not so obvious is the second most important parental obligation: maintaining an overview.

Parents are not only the best at providing an overview;

PLANNING FOR YOUR CHILDREN'S LIVES

they are the only ones who should be doing it. Children have difficulty in the areas of oversight or foresight because at their age they have so little exposure to the world. The providers of programs, services, and products aren't good at oversight and foresight either, because they are too focused on the short term view; for example making sure Sally can read or just simply making a profit. Parents are the ideal overseers and future planners because they are the family historians and they have been given the legal, "omniscient" responsibility for their children. They have a view of not only where each child has come from and where he is headed, but also where the family fits in. All of this is not to say that parents can't delegate or even abdicate this responsibility; some do. I just don't think that the overview function should ever be done, unless by necessity, by a relative stranger.

The selection of programs, products, and services should not be delegated, either. Just as you are what you eat, you are probably the mentor you work with, which makes it critical that you find mentors for your children that you most respect. Of course, you as parent are the penultimate mentor—the person that your child will pattern after most. Next to you, however, is a whole world of interesting and talented people, so in like manner, selecting programs, products, and services should not be delegated.

MANAGING THE SELECTION PROCESS

I believe parents have a lifetime to refine, grow, and strengthen their parenting abilities. After all, once you become a parent, you are a parent for the rest of your life. On the other hand, you are needed most during your children's early years, when your job is complex and demanding, with a great deal

77

CHAPTER FOUR

to do within a limited amount of time. During this period, one of the most important, time-consuming, and challenging duties you have is managing the selection process.

By *selection* I am referring to your choice of schools, after-school programs, summer programs, inter-session programs, and all other specialized programs. In short, everything needed for your child's development. By *selection process*, I mean there is a step by step procedure that you should go through to seek, investigate, research, choose, implement and evaluate programs, services, and products; and by *managing the selection process*, I'm referring to the process of administering these steps.

The problem is that there are so many programs, services, and products available that the search process can be over-whelming — especially for parents whose time available for raising their children is increasingly limited. Having so many choices is a good thing. Not being able to take advantage of this vast array is unfortunate. Searching thoroughly can easily take all of a parent's available time. We may be in an information age, but as it relates to these programs and services information is fragmented, making it very difficult to comparison shop.

■ How Most Parents Select Schools for Their Children

One can only imagine that parents use a strategy of doing the best that they can, and word of mouth is probably popular. Trusted friends, co-workers and neighbors are canvassed, to be sure. We love these people, we trust them, and so we are comfortable following their advice. Chance is probably a large factor. We might overhear a snippet of talk radio, eavesdrop on a water cooler conversation, or see an article in a magazine

PLANNING FOR YOUR CHILDREN'S LIVES

or newspaper. It may sound right and we don't know where else to look, so we jump on it. Time limitations, we suspect, play a major role. How much time do we have to sit next to the phone and call for information, be put on voice mail recordings, and be shunted from one person to the next? When we do call companies and organizations offering programs, services, and products, we are not necessarily getting the unvarnished truth about their offerings. We are also not discovering information relevant to the particulars of our children — how these offerings might apply to them. How long and how costly will it be for us to find out?

As an author and a parent, I've learned a great deal about the selection process. For example, I've taken weeks and weeks of available parental time to try to make a reasonable consumer choice about schools to send my daughter to. In the next chapter, I'll share the numerous strategies available to parents to make this process work.

IMPLEMENTING CHOICES

Hope is the feeling you have that the feeling you have isn't permanent.

– Jean Kerr

Once a program, service, or product selection is made, management responsibility begins with the delegation of authority. For the parent, good management means implementing at least five steps:

1. *Scheduling the program or service.*
You've got to find a way to fit everything in, but take this step very seriously: you don't want to overschedule your child's

79

CHAPTER FOUR

time, leaving him no freedom to think, explore, and develop on his own. You are not running a military operation here! On the other hand, neither do you want to leave too much time on his hands, so that he withers from tedium. There is no blueprint for every child; his thresholds and boundaries are unique to himself. This is where the extensive knowledge gleaned from observing your child comes in handy.

2. *Observing the effects on your children*
A good manager is a keen observer who notices everything. It is very difficult to improve a situation unless someone has been watching closely and carefully noting the causal linkages between actions and outcomes. You are the person who shares a history with your child, and this puts you in an ideal position to do the observing.

3. *Observing the program or service provider at work*
Next to you, the program service provider will be the most consequential element in your child's development. He or she is going to be a surrogate mentor to your child. Bearing this in mind, you need to observe your child's performance in the program and ask yourself, How does this person interact with my child? You should be watching for insights into their character.

4. *Evaluating the child, the service provider, and the context*
Judgment is again important here. Development will take place between the program context, the surrogate mentor, and your child. If your child isn't doing well, it is up to you to distinguish between the influences of all the variables. You are also responsible for outlining a set of expectations to

PLANNING FOR YOUR CHILDREN'S LIVES

guide your child and the service provider. Be prepared for this. You are the guiding light.

5. *Intervening when necessary*

Your child's progress will be hampered if you fail to intervene when necessary to get things back on course. Your child's service provider can be your representative in most situations. However, you will be needed to do the things that the surrogate mentor can't. Don't stress over this now; you'll know what these are when they arise. You'll have to decide to what degree of detail it is appropriate and comfortable to manage what goes on routinely. Will you manage generally or micromanage all the fine points?

■ The More Delegation, the More Teamwork

Management implementation can be difficult for the parent who is constrained by time. If only parents could be omniscient! Many of us can only complete the scheduling, and must leave the implementation to our delegates. We entrust a great deal to others and hope they fulfill our expectations. Placing so much responsibility on individuals outside our immediate family puts extra emphasis on the necessity of good communication between parents and providers and between parents and children. All the parties involved have to work as a team.

There are other issues as well. All children have different abilities and learn at different rates. They will differ in the number of programs they can successfully participate in at any one time. It is a parent's job to discover these preferences in order to create developmental harmony between the programs and the child. Parents must also keep in mind that

CHAPTER FOUR

children in group situations are treated uniformly by teachers, who must rightly concern themselves with giving equal time and attention to each child. Parents should not expect a provider to give their child special privileges or attention in such a situation.

■ Reasons to Delegate

The delegation of parental authority can be an answered prayer or a nightmare. It is a matter for caution and careful consideration. My advice to you is that you proceed carefully.

The primary benefit of delegation is clear: it's a time saver. Your time is in demand. Raising children involves making an enormous time commitment. But what if you have very little of it available? How do you raise happy children then? The answer is delegation.

A further benefit of delegation is that your children will learn new skills that you are unable to teach. Can you teach your child judo or how to play the violin? You probably couldn't, even if you had the free time! There is an infinite number of skills that you may not be an expert in but that your children would benefit by learning. Delegation is a gift to the future when it enriches a child and equips him for a life of action and involvement.

A third good reason to delegate is that you are thereby conserving your energy for duties that cannot be delegated. I've covered a few of these already: maintaining an overview; working with your children to select programs, services, and products; showing up; and giving 100 percent of your attention.

82

PLANNING FOR YOUR CHILDREN'S LIVES

■ The Challenges Inherent in Delegation

I could easily go on and on about the benefits, but what about the difficulties? Even on a good day, delegation can be challenging. Getting it right demands patience and understanding, especially if you're:

✦ *Too Perfectionistic.* Remember what we said about having too many expectations? If you're a perfectionist about delegation, you're toast. You will never achieve perfection in this area. Accept this, scale back your hopes, and move on.

✦ *Too Observant.* Second, if you're both a perfectionist and very observant, you're toast squared. If you notice every little detail, you may go crazy because you can't control them all.

✦ *Too Particular.* Third, if you're a perfectionist, very observant, *and* picky, you're toast cubed. Strike three and batter out! Being particular probably already drives you crazy. Smile if you're thinking at this very moment, "Yeah, that's me."

✦ *Not Accepting Enough.* In delegation, the most challenging thing is accepting what you find and moving forward. There's no room for perfectionism. You must learn to accept what you may perceive as the shortcomings of others. Other people are, by definition, different than you. They reason, perform, and act in a different way. How good are you at accepting these differences in the hope of achieving a greater goal?

83

CHAPTER FOUR

Delegation can also be challenging if you're subject to:

+ *Unclear Communication*. Nearly as difficult as acceptance is clear communication. It's critical to effective delegation, but difficult even among the best of friends. Effective communication is two-way, active, life-affirming, and free from dampening restrictions or hurtful statements.

+ *Unmanaged Expectations*. Another area of difficulty is the management of expectations—yours and other people's. You need to be crystal clear about your own expectations and also aware of the expectations that others have about you.

On paper, these issues seem clear-cut, but in real life they're a muddle: multiple, interconnected, and compounded by other issues. Suffice it to say that, for most people, delegation is too beneficial to forego but a challenge to manage successfully. Fortunately, there are strategies that can help.

DELEGATION STRATEGIES
■ Cast Your Net Wide
Delegate your authority to talented people. Never assume, however, that because an individual is an expert at doing one thing that he is good at doing all things. Keep your expectations realistic. A good piano teacher is worth his weight in gold, but that doesn't mean he is a good character model. Diversify your delegation choices to give your child a balanced experience.

■ Create a List of What You Want to Delegate
Creating a list will help you to clarify what you want to do

PLANNING FOR YOUR CHILDREN'S LIVES

yourself and what you want to delegate to others. A list may open your eyes to what has been right under your nose but you didn't notice because you weren't looking. There's just something about writing things down that gets your mental equipment in motion.

■ Keep Your Expectations Low So They Can Easily Be Surpassed

Set up your delegating plan to succeed in small steps that are easy to accomplish over short periods of time. This enables your expectations to be exceeded. When they are surpassed, be lavish in your sincere praise. This will encourage those to whom you have delegated to proceed enthusiastically in the knowledge that you are a fair and observant manager.

■ Keep Your Mind Open to What's Outside the Box

Grandma may be the best batting coach and older brother the best cook in the family, but you won't know this until you let go your preconceptions. You may not even recognize the brilliance of these skills unless your mind is open to seeing talent where it is not expected.

■ Ask and Your Delegates Shall Be Given to You

Delegating can be easy once you get the knack of it. The secret lies in first establishing what your children like to do and then matching them up with people who can teach these things. Then you don't have to call it parenting or delegating; you can just call it fun. How hard is it to ask an artistic uncle to teach his nephew to draw? If your son shows the slightest interest, his uncle will be easy to persuade, and probably flattered to be asked.

85

CHAPTER FOUR

■ Seek Talent in the Extended Family of Friends and Acquaintances for Delegation: a.k.a. Child-Rearing Support System Map

One important thing a parent can do to facilitate delegation is to understand a hierarchy of parenthood map. It is a simple inventory of the family circle of relatives, friends, and acquaintances. The inventory is arranged by the strength of blood relationships, from the closest relationships immediately below the family on the top of the hierarchy to the weakest blood relationships on the lowest rung of the ladder. By definition, those highest in the hierarchy have the greatest potential to be the most effective parental substitutes. Of course, there are significant limitations in using this hierarchy as a guide to parental delegation. Many families can't delegate parental authority to their close relatives because they live a long distance away. Many family members in our current culture no longer feel much of an obligation to help their relatives. In addition, some of our most devoted and helpful friends are not related to us at all.

The Child-Rearing Support System Map

Parents

Close friends

Brothers and sisters, uncles, aunts, cousins

Foster parents, step parents, teachers, neighbors

Step-brothers, step-sisters, baby-sitters, au pairs, nannies

*All other casual acquaintances and other
intermittent acquaintances*

*All community, state, national, and worldwide
child welfare institutions*

86

PLANNING FOR YOUR CHILDREN'S LIVES

This is a hierarchy structured by values, culture, and context, and so it may vary considerably each time it is applied. What is interesting about it is that it can be used as a framework for formulating a delegation strategy of mothering, fathering, and "othering." In other words, it is a map of child-rearing support system potential for any family.

OTHERING

In our current culture, othering is a key element in many parents' and children's lives because such a large proportion of a child's time is now spent outside the nuclear family. What, more precisely, is othering? It is the relationship between a child and those (nonparents) in closest proximity; for example, neighbors (Hamasaki, 2001). The map of potential child keepers above may also be seen as:

+ An inventory of a circle of relatives, friends, and acquaintances

+ A map depicting the strength of parental and surrogate bonding

+ A social safety net

+ A rank order of trust

+ A rank order of respect

+ A rank order of responsibility

How you see the hierarchy is up to you. I see it as a useful tool to assist in solving problems, understanding delegation issues, or predicting problems. It is an entire child-rearing support system at a glance. What a parent needs to do to make it realistic for her, is to assign specific names to the categories

CHAPTER FOUR

holding places above (adding and subtracting categories as needed); then to arrange these names in a hierarchy that describes her specific reality. For example, if you as parent became seriously ill, requiring hospitalization for a period of three months, how would you arrange this hierarchy and who would you substitute for the roles listed in your hierarchy?

■ **The Mitchells' Telephone Tree**

One example that illustrates the value of this map is an amusing scene from *Dennis the Menace: The Movie*, released a few years ago. If you've seen it, perhaps you remember the scene in which Mr. and Mrs. Mitchell are telephoning potential baby-sitters for Dennis so they can both go on business trips out of town. After just a few moments, the observer quickly realizes that the Mitchells face a continuous stream of rejection as they proceed toward completely exhausting their enormous telephone tree. Dennis is a persona non grata in the neighborhood (translation: a holy terror), so it is not surprising that most people don't want the baby-sitting duty. Sure enough, the scene is portrayed as taking a significant amount of time, as both parents call and call unsuccessfully. Finally Mrs. Wilson, their kindhearted next-door neighbor, agrees to take Dennis in, much to the Mitchells' relief, for there was simply no one else to do the job.

For the Mitchells, having an extensive telephone tree was a necessity, given the kind of son they had (a brat), their specific neighborhood (suburban), the culture of the country they lived in (the U.S.A.), their work responsibilities (as dual bread-winners), their parental responsibility-sharing agreements (equal between the marriage partners, and highly delegated

88

PLANNING FOR YOUR CHILDREN'S LIVES

to others outside the family), the structure of their household (nuclear), and their support system (minimal family and highly fragmented). They were very lucky that they could take advantage of "othering" with their neighbors. Many people are not so fortunate.

The Mitchells' phone tree was nothing more than a map of the same Child-Rearing Support System that I'm asking you to construct on paper as a valuable tool. I certainly have done this before myself, and in fact I still have one, updated for my current circumstances. More than one tree may be constructed for the different situations that will typically be confronted. For example, in addition to extended hospital stays and short-term babysitting, there may be times you need to call upon it for holidays, summer vacations, out-of-town business assignments, long-term absences and disability, and —yes—even a death in the family.

LESSONS WE CAN DRAW FROM THE MAPPING TECHNIQUE
■ A Child-Rearing Support Structure Has Become a Necessity

We now live in a world that necessitates wage-earning parents being separated from their children for extended periods, even when they are still very young. Employers place such great demands on parental time that many former parental functions must be carried out by parental substitutes. The working world imposes demands on parents to leave their children for long hours during the working week, and sometimes on holidays and weekends. Parents would simply not be able to fulfill these demands without a child-rearing support structure.

89

CHAPTER FOUR

■ This Structure Represents Most of Your Child's Life Influences

The diagram is intentionally constructed so that all the components of the support structure of your child are represented. Other influences on children can include pets, books, radio, television, films, and the Internet, but these influences probably remain minimal.

The hierarchy can be seen as a hypothetical structure of living support lying between your child and the world at large. Anything below the parent level is a parental substitute.

■ Mapping Allows Key Issues to Come to the Fore as Parental Reminders

I remember most of my early years of parenting as a blur of outside influences, such as school and career activities. In such a context, having a simple tool such as the Child-Rearing Support System Map with visual reminders would be helpful. Mapping is the perfect system to manage an overview.

■ Delegation Will Require Training

When you delegate your parental authority, remember that while there are many potential parental substitutes, you may consider most to be a barely adequate substitute for all that you do for your children, which means you should delegate very selectively. As in all delegation, it's your responsibility to train those who stand in for you. This training includes time to communicate, witness, practice, master, and test. You should be willing to be patient and accept personal responsibility for having trained your substitutes inadequately when things go wrong. In other words, if delegating your parental authority doesn't work out, chances are that it was your fault for not training your substitutes properly.

90

PLANNING FOR YOUR CHILDREN'S LIVES

■ Trust and Respect Diminish as You Descend Down the Structure

The trust and respect that children have for the people on the list often weakens as you travel down the hierarchy. As trust and respect diminish, so may your children's sense of well-being. How does this work? Without good parenting, children are fated to develop as best they can. Receiving zero parental assistance is the equivalent of growing up blindfolded with your hands tied behind your back. Receiving minimal parental assistance (e.g., having untrustworthy parents who are often absent) means perhaps removing the blindfold.

The lives of foster children as depicted in books (for example, *The Cider House Rules*) give us an insight into the possible effects of inferior parenting. Deprived of significant emotional support from their direct families, foster children are emotionally insecure and fearful of trusting their own capabilities. This means their growth and development is significantly handicapped. They are forced to withdraw to find strength in themselves.

■ Delegating to Individuals High in the Structure Is Ideal

The top positions in the pyramid should be filled by people who live close by, are closely related to you, or are highly trusted by you and your children. Delegating to these folks doesn't require an exchange of money — just friendly requests and thanks or some kind of equitable exchange (e.g., couples who trade babysitting services). Delegation here is not a chore but an act of love. No one thinks they're going out of their way.

■ Delegating to Those in the Middle Is a Calculated Risk

Those who occupy middle positions are contractors who are

91

CHAPTER FOUR

paid money to provide programs, services, and products to your children. These include schoolteachers, baby-sitters, and skilled specialists. Contractors are trained before engaging in contract work. Some may need additional guidance from you to adapt their program to your child. These contractors owe a legal duty to perform their services as described and expected.

■ Delegating to Those on the Bottom Is to Be Done Sparingly

Selecting parental surrogates from far down in the hierarchy is not a good option, because these positions are occupied by institutions that cannot provide the kind of emotional support children need. Additionally, institutions are guided by rules, not by individuals, so it is difficult to find a good fit for a child who has special problems or needs.

A WORD ABOUT TOO MUCH DELEGATION

> *Scientists have been unable to discover the many profound principles that relate the action of mothers, fathers, or siblings to psychological characteristics in the child.*
>
> – Jerome Kagan, *The Nature of the Child*

■ How Much Time Should You Spend with Your Children?

We hear a lot about the magical thing called "quality time." To those parents concerned about the fact that they're not spending enough of it with their children, give yourself a break. The truth is that there isn't a fixed or arbitrary amount of time that you need to spend with your children. Each

92

PLANNING FOR YOUR CHILDREN'S LIVES

family's situation is different. Yes, your children do need your attention and guidance, as often and as regularly as you are able to give it. And you must always be reachable by telephone so that you can be summoned home in an emergency—your children need to know that you're always available to them in time of need. Sometimes they need only the reassurance of hearing your voice on the phone to go contentedly on with some activity.

■ How Little Is Too Little?

Being forced to spend a lot of time away from home to earn a living is a common reality for many people, especially those who live with economic instability. Family sizes continue to dwindle as the number of one-parent homes increases. Today, one in every two marriages ends in divorce. Extended families are no longer living close together. As we have detailed, these trends have all increased the number of parental substitutes, and introduced a host of new challenges.

Some parents out there are so busy that they delegate almost everything. How is a child to really know his parents when most of his time is spent apart from them? What is so troubling about this is that statistics indicate that it is not at all uncommon. Declining parental guidance continues to be a strong trend. Parents are not delegating authority to those close to home, either. They are delegating authority to programs and institutions that can give these parents what they want—structured atmospheres that keep children away from home much of the time. A reasonable amount of delegation can be a great thing in a healthy family, but delegation can be a grave mistake if carried to excess or improperly managed.

CHAPTER FOUR

LISTENING TO YOUR CHILDREN

I wish people who have trouble communicating would just shut up.

– Tom Lehrer

■ Develop Your Communication Skills

One of the most important things you can do for your children, especially if you're delegating a significant amount of parental authority, is to develop your communication skills. This means simultaneously increasing your powers of observation (inflow) and speech (outflow). The concept of simultaneous inflow and outflow is important, because communication with children frequently occurs this way. Yes, it is very hard to listen and speak at the same time, but that is exactly what is required of parents because children don't understand our adult speech protocols.

Of course, the acts of observation and speaking are two entirely different processes. It may be helpful to review the finer points of these differences here, to enable you to become more skilled at both.

■ Children Communicate by Many Means, Adults Mainly by Speech

Communication is not limited to written and spoken words, despite how adults may behave. Children communicate with the full repertoire of their bodies, their senses, and their actions. An observant adult will be able to read a child, who doesn't need to tell you with words that she is upset when she can say it much more eloquently by the volume of her voice or the speed (or lack of it) in her movements.

On the other hand, adults have been conditioned to believe

PLANNING FOR YOUR CHILDREN'S LIVES

that speech is the most efficient way to communicate. Speech is, of course, a very symbolic language that contains many subtleties that children have not had sufficient time to learn. Children understand the basic elements of speech like tone of voice, i.e., intensity, calmness, repetition, but they have very limited understanding of the nuances of many terms and idioms.

Children learn the words, techniques, and meanings of spoken language at a very early age, but their vocabulary is limited so that when they speak, they do so very directly. They don't know nor care too much about sentence structure, so they stick to the basic nouns and verbs that describe what they want to say; and given a choice of how to communicate, speech isn't necessarily their first or most favored means.

■ For Parents, Speech Doesn't Always Speak Best

All of this said, it should be plain that parents should probably not depend totally on speech to communicate with their children. How many of us have witnessed parents yelling at the top of their lungs, at the peak of frustration, struggling in vain to communicate their displeasure, while their children blissfully ignore this exaggerated display? Can we assume that these children are monsters, blatantly defying their parents, or do we conclude that what we are witnessing is a failure to communicate?

I think it is clear that parents have a choice. They can ignore their child's preferred mode of communication and insist that the child use speech; or they can adopt more of their child's favored methods until such time as they have transitioned to a greater use of speech.

CHAPTER FOUR

In my case, I chose to adopt my child's methods, but not before learning a few lessons the hard way. Among other things, I learned that putting my hand on my little girl's head or shoulder meant more to her than thousands of my words to let her know that all was okay. Under my hand, I could just feel all her tensions and needless concerns wash away. A simple smile often had a similar effect, as did lying down next to her on the sand, mud, or the floor where she was playing with her toys, simply observing what she was engaged in so intently.

I also learned that my child was often absorbed in her own world to such an extent that the best way to communicate with her was to use the very objects that she was using as play tools.

■ Children Live in an Alternative Reality

My youngest child may have been able to tell time, but she never understood it the way I did. She understood time as abstraction, and for her time wasn't passing by as it was with me.

Very significant parts of my child's days were spent in an imaginary world that demanded her full attention. Interrupting her reverie in the midst of all her buckets and shovels at the beach, for example, was unthinkable to me because I saw that this would disrupt her entire scheme of organization and peace of mind. So I learned to seek better times for communication, when it would be less disruptive to her peace of mind. This is one reason (in addition to demonstrating common courtesy) why parents should always knock before entering a child's room.

96

PLANNING FOR YOUR CHILDREN'S LIVES

■ Watch What They Do, Not What They Say

In observing your children's behavior, my advice is to listen to their speech but recognize that it should be valued far less than observing their actions. Remember that the work of children is play, and that this means even the use of language is for most children, especially the very young. More often than not, they are trying on words and sounds as they might try on dress-up clothes. They don't stand behind the meaning of these words as much as they are experimenting with them, as they do with everything else, so that they can understand them better.

■ Suspend Judgment

Sages have amusingly proclaimed that you can't talk and chew gum at the same time. Nor can you talk and listen at the same time, I might add. Well, if these things are true, then the same might be said of observation and judgment: they cannot be achieved simultaneously. If you're serious about observing your children's behavior, then it means that you must suspend judgment, so that you can withdraw from taking action that would impede the free flow of information.

One way you can increase your powers of observation is to listen more carefully to your children's questions, and answer them more thoroughly. Ask questions about their questions. Doing this will help you better understand your children's feelings, and you will be training your children by example to ask questions before taking action—a much wiser policy for living, in the long run, than its opposite.

97

CHAPTER FOUR

■ Ask Open-Ended Questions

Don't put too fine a point on the questions you do pose to your children. Remember always that they aren't as sophisticated as you are. Ask open-ended questions that give lots of room for a variety of responses, such as "How's it going?" or "How was your day?" These questions have no right or wrong answers. Consequently, they put a minimum of pressure on everyone concerned. They are innocent, pleasant conversation stimulants, as far as possible from the third-degree, courtroom-type questions so popular with the police and legal professions.

■ Become a Partner-Coach

As you delegate more, it's important that you become a partner-coach to your children. Remember, unless you're directly observing what's happening with your children's programs and service providers, or unless someone keeps you informed, you are deaf and blind to what's happening with your children.

■ Allow for Two-Way Conversations

Make your conversations with your children two-way streets in which you share as much as you can about your day, as well as asking about their day. Do this each day, if even for just a few moments in a private place with each child. Volunteer how your day has been going to give them ideas about what you expect as an answer. Try to get clarification about words used or points made that you don't understand. Don't press for answers and don't be upset if the answers you get bear no discernible relation to your questions. Be patient, pay attention, and provide affirmations to their responses by

98

PLANNING FOR YOUR CHILDREN'S LIVES

letting them know that you're listening. This will improve your relationship with your child as much as it improves your child's communication skills.

Hint: You may have to have these conversations while your child is immersed in playing with something, on the principle that speech with you is probably not yet a very significant element of your child's life, while it is probably the center of yours. In addition, you may have to interrupt your child's fantasy play world in order to talk about things going on that you consider real, but he does not. In other words, don't get upset that your child doesn't give what you believe should be his full, undistracted attention to your talk. Talk may be a distraction to your child's main duty, which is to play. Playing well takes a lot of concentration.

■ Take Notes

Take notes after your conversations out of their presence, perhaps even in a diary so you can think about what is happening as well as look back and analyze your observations over time. Remember to pay close attention to their total communication repertoire rather than just what they have said. Think about what their new actions were. Taking notes allows you to think about and therefore pay close attention to what is really going on in your child's life.

■ At Times, Speak Only When Spoken To

In a classic turnaround of the old saying, it is sometimes better to speak with your children only when invited to. This is very hard to do, it's true, especially for parents who feel it's their role to control and direct. If you can wait for your children to ask you for advice, however, rather than volunteering it,

99

CHAPTER FOUR

you'll be establishing an important precedent and your children will hear more of what you have to say when they're ready to listen.

■ Sustain the Flow and Build Trust

It's important for you to suspend judgment about the responses you get. Nothing will stop the flow of communication faster than using information that you have just received from your child against her. In other words, when they tell you that they have really messed up, don't immediately throw it back in their faces and punish them. It is more important that you understand what your children are saying, meaning, experiencing, feeling, and responding to.

Having respect for your children's confidences means not sharing information they tell you with anyone else, least of all their siblings. Trust is built day by day through many small actions. Keep close tabs on this.

■ Give Your Children the Utmost Respect

Disrespecting children is all too easy to do. They're little, they're not very articulate, and they're very vulnerable to influence. Respect for the stage they are in is what they deserve. While you're at it, respect everything you can that they are involved in as if they were kings and queens, or at least princes and princesses. Here are a few helpful hints:

✦ Request permission to enter their rooms by knocking and asking.

✦ Honor their privacy.

✦ Give them choices instead of orders.

100

PLANNING FOR YOUR CHILDREN'S LIVES

+ Say please and thank you at every opportunity (if you do this consistently, you will never need to say another word to them about having manners and respecting others, including you).

+ Physically get down to their level and speak when your eyes are at the same level or below theirs. Would you feel comfortable speaking with someone twice your height now—say ten to twelve feet tall?

+ Give your children the benefit of every doubt.

+ Don't force situations they are in to conform to your point of view.

+ Step back from controlling their lives. Give your children the space and time to be comfortable and express what's on their minds.

+ Be a friend to your children by putting yourself in their shoes and finding ways to be helpful, no matter how small. For example, give them chores and responsibilities, but volunteer to help them when you can by giving them assistance, especially when they haven't asked for it. Little things go a long way. Ask permission to be helpful before you proceed.

BE SUPPORTIVE, EMPOWERING, AWARE, AND POSITIVE

When I was young there was no respect for the young, and now that I am old there is no respect for the old. I missed out coming and going.

– J. B. Priestley

CHAPTER FOUR

■ Being Supportive and Empowering

The more you delegate parental authority to others and spend less time with your children, the more you will be assuming the traditional role of grandpa or grandma. This is not necessarily a bad thing. The good guys with the white hats have traditionally been grandparents while parents have been the black hat, bad guys. Grandparents would ask permission more, say please and thank you more, pay attention more, bring gifts and tell funny stories to their grandchildren. Kids would shower their appreciation on their grandparents in response. Parents would be shocked, perhaps a touch jealous, and maybe a little resentful. They would say the grandparents were spoiling the kids.

Parents, on the other hand would be the nags, the disciplinarians and the ones who lost their tempers and said mean things. Is it any wonder that children looked forward to being with their grandparents more than they did their parents? Divorced fathers experience a similar phenomenon when they are only allowed or able to see their children on weekends or intermittently. They wind up spending more "quality time" with their children than mom who has the daily responsibility for upbringing.

If you sense that you're more of a grandparent to your youngsters than a parent, milk this for all it's worth. Use it as an opportunity to become a god in your own time to your children. Assume the grandparent role with gusto. Respect them as an angel would his or her charges. Build a solid, non-threatening base of communication with your children by listening to them, using some of the simple suggestions described above. If you do so, when traumatic things happen, they will more likely feel you are their safe harbor.

102

PLANNING FOR YOUR CHILDREN'S LIVES

You want to create an environment in which they tell you nearly everything because they feel that your love is not at risk in any encounter with them. Being supportive doesn't mean being passive in the face of dreadful behavior. You can be strong in your positions to resolve these problems. However, you can't be influentially effective until you've bonded so securely that nothing will shake the foundations of your relationship. When you're in this strong position, it will seem nearly effortless to express your opinions when they are sought out. But first you must prepare the ground to support this position. It's not something that happens overnight.

■ Being Aware

The best audience is intelligent, well-educated, and a little drunk.
— Alben W. Barkley

What is this, an audience or an oil painting?
— Milton Berle

Being aware means paying attention to your children, and this skill is one of the most fundamental that parents must master. There's much more to it than meets the eye. Paying attention is a combination of putting your sensory apparatus on full alert (eyes, ears, nose, hands, brain) and maintaining that status over extended periods of time (years and years); and responding (not reacting) with appropriate measures (or countermeasures) to situations as they suddenly may appear— all this with aplomb (composure, ease, and assurance)!

Awareness is two-thirds of good parenting. Pay attention to your parental awareness role. Awareness will flow from

CHAPTER FOUR

these seemingly simple steps—simple, but not easy. Good, regular communications will help you stay well-informed about what is happening, mindful of what is important/ bothering your children, and knowledgeable about your children's circumstances. Conversely, your children will learn to be aware from your modeling. It will help your children to know what you find important about their situation. Performers rate their audiences too, you know. I always keep a running tease going with my child that keeps her smiling and knowing that I'm paying attention. Her feedback is what I keep a watch on.

■ Standing Watch

Paying attention is, in part, standing watch, something much harder than it looks. Ask any sentry or former sentry about this sometime. There are long periods of no change, punctuated by a few false alarms and unpredictable, short, intense emergency periods. The pattern is deadening. The skill it takes to watch paint dry comes to mind. Observing subtle changes is a skill comparable to seeing in the dark. Sometimes you must look indirectly in order to see more clearly. This is why I suggest taking notes, and then of course, going over those notes many times. Responding to change requires a combination of analysis, judgment, and intuition.

■ Being a Good Audience

Awareness is an important characteristic of good audiences. Good audiences don't miss much. If they are paying attention, they will notice both the obvious and the subtle. They are capable of distinguishing between the mundane and the extraordinary and responding appropriately. When they see

104

something sad, they weep; when they see something mundane, they yawn; and when they see something fabulous, they stand up, hoot, and give an enormous ovation.

■ Being Positive

Progress might have been all right once but it has gone on too long.

– Ogden Nash

Being positive as it applies to planning for your children's lives means being steadfast and encouraging about the future in the face of everything that happens. It's an adult concept. Most children appear to have no concern about being positive. They seem to have been born with it until they get to a point of extreme disappointment, frustration, and discouragement. Being positive is an invisible guide that we follow to propel our adult behavior.

Some call being positive an attitude (for example, the attitude of "I think I can" and "The glass is half full, not half empty"). I think being positive is made up of a group of ingredients that are fundamental for adults to have in order to be able to assist those who are growing up: hope, expectations about a favorable future, an emphasis on silver linings, an encouraging belief, an optimism, an enthusiasm for what's around the corner, a zest for living, an attempt to manage the future with self-fulfilling prophecy, a set of perceptions, an awareness of the constructive possibilities, self-confidence, faith, a knowledge about momentum, a joy in living, and a strategy.

Some adults manage to lose being positive on their way to becoming who they are. That is why I want to furnish this

CHAPTER FOUR

reminder that parents need to be positive with their children, so as to not unintentionally limit or extinguish a significant motivation for living.

■ Having a Future Orientation

Being positive concerns the future. The most interesting thing about the future is that it's not real. The future is only made up of possibilities and probabilities. The present is all that is real, although the (immediate) future is just a heartbeat away. How should we deal with concepts that are not real? The future is not even inevitable, although some people we call fatalists believe it is. The future only seems imminent because of our forward momentum, i.e., what we are doing this very minute is very likely to continue on into the next minute. How should we deal with concepts that are neither real nor inevitable? Are we determinists because we believe that the future is malleable? You bet we are.

Most of our future lies in our brains, but we need to realize that the future is very different to children than it is to adults. Ask a child about the future and mainly you get bewilderment. Ask an adult about the future and you also get bewilderment, in addition to a mixture of hunches, expectations, and projections.

Why should we be positive with our children as concerns their future? Because our children have more future before them, and therefore face more limitless possibilities than we do. We as parents have a far different, more limited future, primarily focused on probabilities. When we are in their presence as mentors, we must remember not to be confused by whose future we're planning for. We need to be positive because there are two major barriers to our children's future

106

PLANNING FOR YOUR CHILDREN'S LIVES

that parents can influence: resources and vision. Resources are all things that enable children to get to any future they desire, and they include genetic makeup, education, skill, learning tools, attitude, health, and wealth. We can influence a good number of these components quite easily. Vision is an intangible but critical component in opening the unlimited possibilities of the future. By being positive, parents can help their children to (1) understand what the future is; (2) envision the possibilities of the future; and (3) take down the barriers that inhibit its view.

■ It's All about Your Style

Your particular style of being positive is important. Two factors should be kept in mind. First, growing up is a process of taking innumerable steps, a number of them in the wrong direction, and then making course corrections. It's a progressive process of making small improvements to perfect future actions. We know we won't ever get perfect behavior, but that shouldn't stop us from practicing. Second, being a parent is difficult when you can clearly see in hindsight what was not plain to anyone, including yourself, beforehand. How do you present your insights to your children with 20-20 hindsight? Here are a few helpful suggestions:

✦ *Lighten up.* Employ charm and humor when you can. Smile. Be friendly. Joke around. Tease and tickle. Put your hand on their shoulders when you speak so they can feel your warmth and sincerity. Think of humor as the sugar that makes lemonade a delightful drink, and if humor is the sugar, being positive is the ice that makes the drink go down so refreshingly.

107

CHAPTER FOUR

✦ *Don't be dogmatic.* I can be dogmatic about this in advising you because you've sought my advice by reading this book. On the other hand, you can rarely, if ever, be dogmatic to your children, even when they ask. What is dogmatic? Insisting on things. Don't do it. Suggest instead. Provide options. Broaden the view. Lower the barriers that prohibit a view of the possibilities.

✦ *Assume you don't know everything.* We all know this isn't true, because you probably do (know everything). Give your children a break, however. Maybe there are mitigating circumstances, other factors you haven't considered in everything that happens. This assumption will keep your eyes and ears open, even when your tendency is not to. Remember, respect is paramount. *Whenever you feel the urge to pontificate, just think of another question to ask* (especially about their questions). Ask questions instead of demanding obedience.

✦ *Don't follow your own logic exclusively.* Seek to understand your child's point of view. This is good advice in all communications.

YOUR VALUES AND AGENDA

Your values are so deeply ingrained that you can't see them. Your values and your agenda are what got you to where you are today. You may not be proud of all of these, but you believe in them, which is why you're holding on to them wherever you go.

Your values and agenda are in every story you tell, every declarative statement you utter, every joke you tell, and every choice you make. Your children will pick up on this.

108

PLANNING FOR YOUR CHILDREN'S LIVES

They can't help but do it. Your values and agenda will be all around them all the time—not smothering them, we hope.

These values of yours will inevitably become a foundation for your children to jump off into the future from. The thing is, your children will already know what your values are without your having to tell them. (Actually you have already told them, only you may not have recognized that telling them was what you were doing when you were doing it.)

I've said this before and I'll now repeat it. Don't assume that your children agree with your values and your agenda, or even understand them. You came to your values and agenda during a lifetime of living. They haven't gotten there yet, and no matter what you do they'll come to their own conclusions anyway.

A SUMMARY OF CHAPTER FOUR

Children have never been good at listening to their elders, but they have never failed to imitate them.

– James Baldwin

This chapter has been about the essence of parenting—understanding your children so that you can plan for their lives. I've tried to present the case that children are really different from adults. They have their own agendas and they are in their own world—a world that is every bit as challenging and demanding of concentration as the one we adults occupy. Although we have been there, we aren't there any more and we probably have forgotten more than we remember.

Once we understand the distinctions between childhood and adulthood, my hope is that we will be better able to handle parenthood.

CHAPTER FOUR

All that being said, my advice remains then: Scale back. Back off. Lighten up. Stand down. Cool it. Be patient. Give them time. Don't give a brain transplant to your children. Be a friend, not the führer. You are influencing them anyway, so don't try so hard. Just being near them so that they can see you is almost enough. Don't worry, they'll notice you—in fact, probably far more than you want them to. You don't want to change their behavior so much as you want them to make good choices. Teach them how to make good choices, but let them make the choices. There's a big difference. Just be yourself and let them be themselves.

ASSIGNMENT FOR CHAPTER FOUR

Find a substitute for your child and practice your parenting on it. It can be animate or inanimate, related or unrelated. Your family pet might do, or even someone else's child. Use this substitute to try all your new ideas on before you proceed to use them on your child. Start by taking notes in observing routine behavior. Proceed to greater complexities when you have convinced yourself that you can understand the rules governing its behavior. This will put you in the right frame of mind for parenting your own child. You are now the matador in the ring. Before you put your life on the line, you must first understand the nature and behavior of the bull.

CHAPTER 5

Arming Yourself First: Your Attitudes and Strategy

What you have when everyone wears the same play clothes for all occasions and is addressed by nickname, expected to participate in Show and Tell, and bullied out of any desire for privacy, is not democracy; it is kindergarten.

– Miss Manners (Judith Martin)

A college professor of mine once stood in front of our class and announced, "People are more the same than they are different." Perhaps he meant something entirely unlike what I understood, but ever since, I have gagged on the idea and spat it back up. It just won't go down. In retrospect I think this is one of those statements that is both true and false, although my hunch is it's more false than true.

PEOPLE ARE MORE DIFFERENT THAN THEY ARE THE SAME

I will never have any way of definitively proving my belief, but I have a strong feeling about it. My life experiences, for one, tell me that people are very different from one another. I have never met two people with the same personality, for example.

I can agree that people are more the same than different if you look at physical functions such as breathing, yawning,

CHAPTER FIVE

and the like. Pathologists, paleontologists, and hairdressers would probably agree. All humans share the same emotional needs: recognition, love, and support. Anthropologists, sociologists, and matchmakers would probably agree here too. But when it comes to preference, skill, ability, focus, and purpose, people have what I consider to be enormous differences from one another. These are major differences of type, not just degree. I would never make some of the choices I see my friends making. I would never do some of the things that I see many people do, for any reason. And why is it that some people seem to sit down to something and just effortlessly proceed, while others try to do the same and miserably fumble?

■ The Development Paradox: We're All Taught As If We Were the Same

You agree with what I'm saying because it's true for your life experiences too, don't you? Okay—if you don't, just humor me for now. Let's say for argument's sake that my professor was wrong. Let's agree for the moment that people are very, very different from each other. Now, if this is true, why is it that we're all treated the same when we get into school? I'm sure you've wondered about this before, once when *you* went through it, and then when you witnessed your children and maybe by now your grandchildren going through it. Here's what I recall thinking to myself at the time: Why do teachers insist on pushing square pegs into round holes? Why do they try to turn the mighty Mississippi into a babbling brook? Is it all coming back to you now?

I'm sure there are several reasons why teachers operate this way. Teachers insist on some things for their own convenience that are perfectly reasonable, such as cues for learning all the

112

ARMING YOURSELF FIRST: YOUR ATTITUDES AND STRATEGY

different names of students in class. Nicknames facilitate this for some teachers. I've been a teacher before, so I understand that it's much easier to present one story to thirty students than a different story to each one. If you want to give up not just all your class time but all your free time as well, go for the thirty stories. I also understand that the equal time rule reigns supreme in the classroom: every paid customer is entitled to exactly five minutes of your time as teacher, no less and no more, even though five minutes is too much for some and not enough for others. Fair is fair. We live in a democracy, after all.

■ In School, Which One Is Your Child?

On the other hand, there's no getting around some of the stark facts that present themselves to teachers, such as the following:

+ Brilliant, charismatic, and responsive children govern the class (e.g., children such as the *Peanuts* characters Linus and Schroeder).

+ Domineering children demand attention, while shy ones shrink away from it. Can a teacher ignore the *Peanuts* character Lucy?

+ Verbally expressive children are favored over those who express themselves best on paper and those who don't express themselves at all (a la the *Peanuts* character Sally).

+ Attractive, well-organized, neat, and clean children (that is, children unlike the *Peanuts* character Pig Pen) excel in class.

+ Well-behaved children (some people term them zombies, a.k.a. Stepford children) do better in class. Smart aleck

CHAPTER FIVE

kids have a rough time. This, we suspect, is why so many girls get much better grades than boys do.

✦ It's always a balancing act between the learning styles of children and the various teaching methods. Some children will learn the lesson very easily, others will learn it only with great difficulty, and still others won't learn it at all. Unfortunately, teachers usually select the methods that best suit themselves rather than the learning styles of their pupils.

✦ Nice guys finish last in class (like the *Peanuts* character Charlie Brown).

✦ Once a student falls behind the rest of the class, catching up is a big problem. Hence, conforming to the norm is very important.

✦ Often there are just a few students with a monopoly on the favored traits, and a handful of others who are problematic. The majority of students will fall somewhere in the middle.

To reiterate, there are many differences among children. When I was a teacher, I saw a tremendous array of responses to every idea I presented. I consistently got the full gamut of responses from those who got it, those who got only part of it, those who didn't get it, those who didn't care one way or another, those who looked at me but weren't paying attention, and those who weren't paying attention at all.

■ **If Your Child Isn't One of the Favored Few, Then What?**
First of all, the awful truth. Unless you live in Garrison Keillor's Lake Woebegone, where all the children are above

114

average, the chances are that your child is not one of the favored few in class described above.

Secondly, do not despair! This isn't necessarily bad for your child, but it can be a source of concern to *you* as you gaze in bewilderment at her report card. You must remember that teachers use just one standard to grade all their pupils. The instructor asks himself: Is she learning the material presented to her in the manner and at the pace the school system has determined to be optimal? This despite the fact that children are (we think) quite different from one another and thus vary considerably in their responsiveness to the lessons.

Third, if you are okay with her marks and you believe that her progress is fine given who she is, spend some time reassuring her and letting her know it's all right to be herself, despite what her teachers think.

Fourth, if you are not okay with her performance in school, you might consider targeting what you believe to be her problem areas and getting her enrolled in a remedial class or engaging a tutor. But! Before you do anything, remind yourself that she is not necessarily going to be happy with anything in which you get her involved. You may first have to work with her to understand her response to her school situation. When you have a better picture, ask for her opinion about your remedy before proceeding.

■ Doing Well in Life, Not School, Is the Goal

I'll let you in on a secret of great parenting: *Respect your children above all else.* They have different preferences, aptitudes, and abilities than you, as indeed your adult friends and acquaintances do. They have different needs than you do. Your appreciation may not be comprehensive enough. Tread

CHAPTER FIVE

lightly. Give them more credit than you think might be right. Address small issues first. Generally know exactly what you're looking for before you go seeking out a program, service, or product. Know that you may find what you're looking for in many different kinds of programs, not just in the ones directly addressing what you see as problem behavior requiring a remedy. Find out which kind of student your child is, in class and out, and respond accordingly. Let the program you fashion follow the purpose you intend to accomplish.

■ First Find the Real Problem

A note of caution: If your son is unbearably shy, it makes sense to predict that he will not function well in classes where his teachers reward the opposite behavior. What might help him is a program that prepares children to deal better with situations that exacerbate shyness. This course of action is good common sense, but if you don't realize that shyness is the cause of his falling grades, what then? You may be racking your brain and spinning your wheels for quite some time before you take effective action. Because, you see, his shyness may not present itself in your home as it does in the classroom, and thus you won't know about it unless you witness it for yourself, or his teacher is moved to share the information with you. The challenge to recognizing problems is that they are usually subtle or well camouflaged, and many problems go unnoticed by parents who only spend a small amount of time with their children, as is the case with many of us these days. So defining the problem may take a while.

■ A Nail Is Not Just a Nail, It's a Connector

If you ask a child to draw you a picture of a hammer and a

116

ARMING YOURSELF FIRST: YOUR ATTITUDES AND STRATEGY

nail, that's what she will present you with. On the other hand, if you ask a child to draw you a picture of something that will connect two pieces of wood together, you'll receive a wide array of responses. You may get a blanket covering the wood, wood in a backpack, or wood glued together—all legitimate methods of connecting wood. This is classic "thinking outside the box," made possible by the way you frame the question. Creative professionals know this, and parents need to know it too. I can't think of a profession that requires more resourcefulness than parenting. Yes, parenting is a profession—a lifetime one, up to now practiced principally by mothers.

Why is the framing of questions important? Because the way you define the problem you are trying to resolve is the way in which it will be resolved. If this just sounds like doubletalk, bear with me for a while.

If you ask, for example, what kind of shyness problem your son has, you've had two important proconceptions, both of which could be off the mark. For one, you've limited the answers or solutions to questions of shyness. Shyness may not be the problem itself; it may be just a symptom of a problem. Secondly, you've concluded that shyness is a problem and not just a trait. Shyness may not be a personality trait you think is beneficial for your son to have, but this could be more a problem for you than your son. He may be perfectly content being shy.

■ Is Shyness Really the Problem?

Before assuming that shyness is a problem and charging ahead, you need to be sure that your son has what you think he has *and* that your solution is appropriate. To the point, if you're wrong and shyness is not the problem you think it is, you could do a lot of damage. This could be costly to everyone

CHAPTER FIVE

involved. Let's follow this example. You think it's shyness because your son is nonverbal in situations when everyone else speaks up. In other words, "nonverbalness" is a symptom or indicator of shyness. If you conclude that it is, and jump on shyness as the problem, your next move will probably be to look for the causes of the shyness so that you can formulate an appropriate solution.

Let's say you've concluded that his shyness is a sibling problem. Your son's older brothers have intimidated him so much that he's turned into a wimp. You want him to stand up for himself instead of letting them walk all over him all the time. You see this as a problem that could lead to all sorts of other problems in his relationships and in group situations throughout his life, i.e., in his career, in dating, and in marriage. You decide to enroll him in a karate class to bolster his self-confidence. You figure if he builds his skill to a certain level, he won't let others bowl him over because he'll have an equalizer to defend himself. Right? Wrong.

■ **What's Wrong with This Picture?**

Let's look at this more closely. Let's say that what appeared to be shyness is not the problem you thought it was. Your son's nonverbal behavior is not a symptom of shyness, but an excellent strategy he's started employing as an attention-getting technique in a large family. In a group of loud, domineering people (his brothers and perhaps his father as well), he's discovered that being opposite works in attracting attention to him because it is in such contrast. Attracting attention gets him more sympathy. This in turn gets him compensation in the form of favored treatment in the use of the family resources— for example, bathroom time, a private bedroom, and other

118

ARMING YOURSELF FIRST: YOUR ATTITUDES AND STRATEGY

things. In addition, he's discovered that when he's quiet, he can listen and observe more carefully what's going on. This enables him to better prepare for things to come. All of his choices have actually been very astute, and will probably lead to important skills he'll have for the rest of his life. He enjoys his karate class. It does give him more self-confidence, but it doesn't change his nonvocal strategy at all, because he's getting too much of a payoff to change.

■ A Problem May Be Just a Symptom of the Real Problem

Let's look at some other common examples of this situation. If a person has a heart attack, what can you conclude? Well, for one, you might conclude immediately that this person needs surgery to correct a physical problem. Right? Not so fast. The physical problem may just be a symptom of poor diet and lack of exercise. Right? Not so fast. The person could have been given the psychological shock of a lifetime. Perhaps his spouse just won the lottery.

Maybe you're getting my point now. A problem may not be a problem, just a symptom or indicator of the real problem. To solve a problem effectively, you need to get closer to the root of it instead of working on the symptoms, which may easily be misinterpreted as indicators of something they really aren't. Solutions can be found to all sorts of phenomena. The problem is, only solutions to the real problems will solve the problem. Confusing? You bet. To help you sort this out, it may help to study the following diagram, using another example taken from the array of typical childhood issues. When you have finished looking at the example, you might try this analysis technique on a few problem situations now facing you with your children.

119

CHAPTER FIVE

■ A Hypothetical Situation Involving a Boy Named John

John's parents think he needs to enroll in a sports activity in which he already excels (swimming) so that he can build more self-esteem. This, in turn, will reduce his insecurity around others and apparent need for excessive attention, which he attracts by his smart aleck back talk behavior with anyone and everyone around him.

Initial Perceptions (Your First Reading)

Problem: Smart aleck behavior

Symptom: Back talk

Cause: Insecurity, need for attention

Solution: Self-esteem building programs, swimming

Instead of rushing to judgment, John's parents follow the advice in this book and, upon further reflection, decide to enroll John in a social communication program. They believe that his back talking, smart alecky behavior is really a reflection of his lack of communication skills. He needs to learn how to read the messages other people are transmitting and respond appropriately. John interprets some behavior of his peers and the adults around him as hostility and a lack of respect directed toward him, instead of innocent inopportune expressions directed at no one in particular. He has chosen to deflect and redirect back to the peers and adults what he believes to be their messages to him, not realizing that there are more effective ways to handle the situations in which he finds himself.

Alternatives to Initial Perceptions (Your Reconsideration)

Problem: Responding to perceived hostility and lack of respect

120

ARMING YOURSELF FIRST: YOUR ATTITUDES AND STRATEGY

Symptom: Back talk
Cause: Ignorance of better communication alternatives
Solution: Social communication program

What I've presented here is a technique that you might find useful in examining what's going on in your own family. Used correctly, it may eventually help you formulate a plan of action for dealing with problems when they arise.

BIG PICTURE CONSIDERATIONS

Live so that when your children think of fairness and integrity, they think of you.

– H. Jackson Brown, Jr.

■ Direct Your Child's Character, Not Her Behavior

Lengthy debates can take place about the effectiveness of various character- and behavior-shaping methods by parents. The reality is, most parents spend the majority of their time and energy trying to control their children's behavior in the short term, forsaking changes that are more lasting and will have more significance in the long run.

Earlier, I made the point that you need not do very much to influence your children long-term. Just being yourself around them is plenty. Your children will see and choose for themselves which behaviors they want to emulate. I suggested that you look in a mirror to see what they may become. This book makes the point that many parents in the present day have found it necessary to spend more time away from their children than ever before. Substitutes are increasingly standing in for parents, and these individuals will become secondary role models for children, depending upon how much time they spend with them.

121

CHAPTER FIVE

■ What's Going into the Pot?

The social "physics" of these points are plain. Whomever your children spend a significant amount of time with will influence the shaping of their long-term character. Generally, the greater the time spent, the more influence there will be. To use a cooking metaphor, all ingredients added to a pot will contribute to the final outcome of soup, but the ingredient that makes up the largest proportion will become the soup's predominant flavor. In the case of upbringing, the key factor in determining your child's long-term character will be the time spent with you and your designated substitutes.

If you want to intentionally influence your children's character, then you need to consider these three questions: (1) How much time do you have to spend with your children throughout their formative years? (2) What can you be doing about your own consistent behaviors, habits, and preferences? and (3) Have you been paying attention to the most influential character traits of your stand-ins?

It's not so much what you say to your children as what you do that makes the biggest difference. Don't look to too many programs, services, and products to be of assistance in this department, unless you are prepared to provide them consistently for years and years. One day in church, so to speak, will not reform a sinner or make a preacher. Devoting your energy to working on the permanent reshaping of your own character will probably be more effective than working on the development of your children's character, but you will have to pay attention to both.

You must also be vigilant for clues in your observation of the big picture: the general behavior of the nation, state, and

122

ARMING YOURSELF FIRST: YOUR ATTITUDES AND STRATEGY

community in which you live; the policies of the institutions you send your children to (school, church, and recreation providers); the books, TV programs, and movies your children take in.

Remember that short-term behaviors are far easier to fix and change than character. With this in mind, you should spend more time attending to what your children are being exposed to every day, rather than worrying about the passing storms that occur in their lives from time to time.

GOOD TRAITS AND MISSING TRAITS

> *A boy can learn a lot from a dog; obedience, loyalty, and the importance of turning around three times before lying down.*
>
> – Robert Benchley

Traits are qualities that distinguish people. They can be inherent, inherited, or developed. I'm focusing on the developed traits here. I see traits as the components of character—not so broad a consideration as the totality of a person's being. It's logical that you might hear someone say, "Her character is admirable, but she has the alarming trait of confronting people with brutal honesty."

■ Many Traits Make Up One's Character

Nearly everything I have said about how character is formulated over the years can be said about the development of traits. However, due to their being just a component of character, adding, subtracting, or modifying traits may fall more easily within the range of a workable program. A person's character

CHAPTER FIVE

might not be fully known until you've been around her for, say, a decade. A certain trait of that person, on the other hand, might be sensed almost immediately.

Whereas we might consider a person's overall character as a single entity, we refer to a whole raft of component traits— larger than life, middling, and minor — when going over someone's characteristics. What are some of the positive ones among these traits? The following come to mind: honesty, integrity, loyalty, obedience, a sense of humor, fairness, kindness, gentleness, maturity, sensitivity, balance, openness, flexibility, and sensibility, to name a few. The list is endless.

■ How Long Do Good Traits Take to Develop?

Can a sense of fairness be developed in almost anyone? I'd have to say yes, there is a good probability of accomplishing it. But how long would it take? That would depend on the individual. Can you develop a sense of fairness by just observing the behavior of people nearby? Probably, yes. Can you develop a sense of fairness in a relatively short period, such as in the course of a one-year program at school? Probably, yes. But just how strong will this trait be after a year of development? That will vary with the individual and the training program.

■ Children Don't Take on Traits Intentionally

It should be noted that our children assimilate traits from external sources. Many such traits are "contagious" to children, for children are impressionable. How much impact a trait will have on a child with varying amounts of exposure is a matter of great conjecture. Moreover, how long and how well a trait will stick with a child, once picked up, is worth

124

ARMING YOURSELF FIRST: YOUR ATTITUDES AND STRATEGY

considering. Children are notoriously unpredictable about what they'll hold on to and what they'll discard after a brief interval.

■ Trait-Developing Institutions Are Having Less Influence

Churches and temples have traditionally played the role of developing the character traits of their parishioners, including children. This worked well in the past for character building, which requires long-term and consistent exposure to good role models in a stable family and community environment. In recent decades, however, consistent attendance at houses of worship has declined, and with this shift has come the loss of an important contribution in the upbringing of our children.

Disruptive trends have exacerbated this situation, chief among them an increase in fragmented lifestyles. We've become such a mobile society that we relocate, on average, every three years. Moving so often makes it difficult for us to reconnect with trait-building support systems. With one in every two marriages ending in divorce, and new partners entering our lives, our families are constantly being restructured. Family sizes are decreasing with these changes, so that we can no longer depend upon family members to share in role modeling.

I don't believe that the need for character development has diminished. On the contrary, social critics everywhere have raised the alarm that serious problems in this area persist in our society. Alternative solutions to fit the social challenges of our present day are what many are now seeking. In the context of current trends, how do we parents develop the good traits and supply sources for the missing ones that we see our children need? To whom do we turn?

125

CHAPTER FIVE

HABITS GOOD AND BAD

One has to grow up with good talk in order to form the habit of it.

— Helen Hayes

Habits can form very quickly, for habit formation is much easier than the building of character traits. Popular self-improvement books on the market say three weeks is all you need to create a habit. Who knows whether this is true? Does this mean, for example, that if we starve ourselves for three weeks we can lose weight in a weight-loss program and keep it off forever, because we're committed to a habit? Of course it doesn't; that would be ridiculous. In the case of dieting, we know that diets usually aren't sustainable because the motivation of the benefits of weight loss is not strong enough to overcome a whole host of other issues that may be causing our extra weight.

On the other hand, what we do know from experience is that trait formation may take years—a much longer period than is necessary for habit formation. Although we don't know much of the how and why, we do know that habits are regular, repetitive, nearly unconscious actions. They're the routines, daily patterns, and conventions that we follow. When in doubt, we resort to them to pull us through, which is why they can be so valuable. After a while, habits become customary.

■ Getting Rid of Habits Takes Longer Than Forming Them

Hmmm, you say. Could habit formation be thought of as a technique to train children? Could it be useful as a strategy

ARMING YOURSELF FIRST: YOUR ATTITUDES AND STRATEGY

in selecting programs, services, and products for children? The answers are yes it can and no it may not.

Programs, services, and products may fulfill needed functions in your children's lives; there's no doubt about that. We also know that habit formation is what we hope will happen when our children are involved in beneficial new programs. What we don't know enough about is what motivates our children, what sustains their interest, what deep-seated needs they need fulfilled, and a whole host of other complexities that make us human. About all we do know is that if the program, service, or product "fits" our children, habit formation may be a quick thing and a darn useful one at that. Let's keep it in mind then, as a good possibility.

What we're more concerned about here is the tail wagging the dog. Sometimes our habits become so consuming that they begin to master us, instead of the other way around. Have you ever tried to break a bad habit, such as not being able to keep a secret, falling asleep in the middle of a long presentation, or failing to signal when you're changing lanes in traffic? Bad habits and good, by their very nature, preclude other behavior. Also, unwanted habits may take a good bit longer to break than their period of formation, the mythical three weeks.

NEEDED SKILLS AND NOT-SO-NEEDED SKILLS

Status quo. Latin for the mess we're in.

– Jeve Moorman

Skill is the ability to do something well. It's a level of proficiency that distinguishes random acts from deliberate, consistent, and controlled behavior.

127

CHAPTER FIVE

■ Children Are Born with a Minimum of Skills

When it comes to skills, children are born with a few valuable ones such as attracting attention when they aren't happy, consuming food, and discharging waste. Everything else that they'll need to excel in the world, they'll need to learn. In other words, the status quo for them is not good enough to build a life upon.

In selecting programs, services, and products for your children, you're probably keenly aware of many of the major skills your children need to acquire to reach the next level of successful maturation. Alternatively, you may be seeking to help your child overcome some physical or other handicap that's holding her back. You may also be seeking special skills for your child to learn that will supplement the common skills most of us need to get by.

■ Skill Mentoring Is Ideal for Delegation

Skills are what many program providers deliver. They can be acquired relatively easily compared with character traits. Skills also don't have the moral component that traits frequently do. Proficiency at skills depends more on practice than anything else. It is almost the perfect responsibility to delegate to a substitute, who may have more time, better teaching ability, and better tools than you do to transfer what is necessary to your children. You, as parent, should get into the habit of calling a skill a skill. This will remind you that it need not be as traumatic as other kinds of training. Training can be short-term and relatively low-cost.

128

ARMING YOURSELF FIRST: YOUR ATTITUDES AND STRATEGY

TWEAKING THE MISSISSIPPI

Wild horses make the best colts.

– Themistocles

I learned the deep significance of the term "hubris" and its opposite, "humility," in reading a composition by John McPhee entitled *The Control of Nature*. The book is a collection of stories about how men at different times and places have tried and failed to bring nature under control. I was especially moved by a story about how the Army Corps of Engineers has tried but has yet to really succeed at rerouting the Mississippi River around New Orleans. Hubris is the excessive pride and arrogance that men have persistently displayed in trying to control the awesome forces of nature.

■ What If You've Got a Wild Horse? (Maybe All Kids Are Wild Horses)

Hubris also comes to mind when we think of parents who try and fail to harness the forces of nature that govern the children in their charge. Perhaps hubris is too strong a term. Ignorance may describe it better. Though there are plenty of instructional materials available about raising children, your particular young ones didn't come with any. If they had, the very first rule would have been this: Do not to try to overcome the underlying forces within your child that govern his behavior. His sweet and innocent appearance conceals a powerful, independent force that lies hidden deep within his molecular web. My advice is to respect this force. Know that it is there and act accordingly.

129

CHAPTER FIVE

■ Become a Tweaking Parent

Your greatest chance for success as a parent is usually going to be as ambassador rather than head of state or chief prosecutor. But tweaking—that wonderful modern term for creating slight adjustments to make something work better— now, that's more on the scale of expectations you should be aiming for.

Listen to the judo master who says that, in order to defend yourself from your opponent, you must use the force of your opponent's punches to disarm him. Grab the arm that was on its way to your jaw and help it go in the direction it was aimed while simultaneously stepping out of its way. Once out of its way, direct its force into a disarming movement. In this light, if you have a wild horse, be thankful. The majority of work ahead of you has already been done. You won't have to do much to light a fire under one to initiate action. Wild horses are spirited children with an attitude . . . full of energy, blazing speed, and independence. Actually, I think kids are mostly all wild horses, don't you? What are you going to do with someone like that? These are the bright ones, the supertalented ones, the ones who will make something great happen in their lives. If this doesn't excite you, seek help.

More to the point, for wild horses you need to find programs that will challenge their capabilities and stimulate them as they journey in the wilderness. For a wild horse, you need a wild horse coach—one who understands the breed and reverberates in sync. Work with them, baby. Work with them. The rewards will justify your efforts.

130

ARMING YOURSELF FIRST: YOUR ATTITUDES AND STRATEGY

SEEK AND CONNECT

Even if you're on the right track, you'll get run over if you just sit there.

– Will Rogers

In finding your children's programs, services, and products, I think you should use a "seek and connect" method instead of a "being sought after and destroyed" approach. Do you like being sought after, or would you rather be the seeker? By this I mean, do you thrive on junk mail? Do you wait by the phone for salespeople to call? Do you eagerly stay up till all hours of the night waiting for the next batch of commercials? Do you buy newspapers and magazines just for the ads? Have you hugged a billboard today?

■ Proactive Is the Only Way to Be

What's wrong with these images? What do they have in common? If you said it's that, in each of them, someone else is seeking to find you, you were right. If you have plenty of time to wait for the right program to come along, then this may be a good approach for you to follow. If you don't have much time to spend on finding good programs for your children, you need to know some of the basics about seeking and connecting.

■ The Basics of Seeking and Connecting

✦ *You have to find good programs; they won't find you.* Spend 99 percent of your available time on the search and the rest on connecting. Be aggressively proactive. It seems to

131

CHAPTER FIVE

be a principle akin to gravity that good programs must be well hidden.

✦ *Things are rarely what they seem.* Look under the hood. Kick the tires. You may find the best programs in unexpected places. If they say white, you should be thinking that they really mean green. You have to be a good detective. What are they really saying? What aren't they saying?

✦ *Advertising about a program will be minimal, if not nonexistent.* Advertising costs a fortune and good programs don't want to spend their fortunes on advertising, so accept as fact that they were essentially undiscovered until you found them. By minimal, I mean that even when you see an ad for a program that interests you, you won't be able to tell much from the ad content about what's being offered. There's little or nothing about cost or availability, age limitations, and other caveats; little or nothing about the instructors, the program's longevity, and the schedule of offerings; and little or nothing about the program philosophy, the number of enrollees, and what they've learned in the past. Shall I go on?

✦ *The brochures, emails, and flyers will bear little relationship to reality.* I'm not saying they're a pack of lies, just that there are probably many omissions. Providers create handouts as a form of shorthand to describe program content and some specifics, but they leave many questions unanswered.

✦ *At first, your old ways of thinking may be blinding you.* Have you ever noticed that, once you learn about something new, all of a sudden you see it everywhere? So the difference in today vs. yesterday could be you!

132

ARMING YOURSELF FIRST: YOUR ATTITUDES AND STRATEGY

✦ *Ask about a free trial.* Were you one of those who discovered five to ten years into your marriage what your spouse was really like?

✦ *Don't stop seeking when you've found something; just change your strategy.* Sometimes resting is more effective than toiling. Did you ever try to remember something that wouldn't come to mind, only to find that after you had given up and relaxed it came to you? Seeking and connecting is a lot like that. As in the way that things that are wrong with something you've drafted on paper don't appear to you until you've sent it out to someone? Life is like this, so don't assume your seeking is over when you think it's over.

✦ *Tell everyone with a pulse what you're seeking, and only believe about 1 percent of the story they tell you.* Being resourceful is having the confidence that something is there when everyone says it isn't, being able to read between the lines, and seeing gold when everyone else sees thin air. Knowing what you seek before you begin searching makes all the difference in the world.

✦ *Make a pest of yourself.* Ask questions until the cows come home. Have you noticed that nothing happens until a question is asked? It's really an art form. Lawyers train endlessly to ask questions in such a manner that their desired response is the result. How many times have you heard the lame response "I didn't tell you because you never asked"?

✦ *Keep your eye on the ball.* Avoid being distracted. Keep picturing how the program may benefit your child.

CHAPTER FIVE

Okay, had enough? Good. But, since you're not expecting more, here are a few other suggestions.

PAPER AND PENCIL BEFORE BOW AND ARROW

Start slow and taper off.

– Walt Stack

How many times have you heard people say that they hate to plan? They love being spontaneous. That's fine, except that it can be very expensive. If you can afford it, that's marvelous. Planning is more cost-effective than spontaneity. People who plan usually wind up being spontaneous, too; they just start from a position that's much more intelligent.

A plan gives you a base to compare choices with, a backup plan to go with in case your other ideas don't pan out, and an overview reference by which to better judge every part of the puzzle. You're less in the dark. A plan doesn't need to be elaborate, but it does need to be on paper.

■ Get Everyone Involved in Planning

Don't connect before you seek. Don't seek before you plan. Don't plan alone. Get your children involved all the way up to their elbows. Planning is a process whereby all the stray, knee-jerk, untoward, impractical, and bad ideas must be proposed and discarded before the good can emerge. Doing this on paper (or computer) is a lot less expensive and time-consuming than going ahead and doing it in actuality right off.

Of course, you must remember that you and your charges aren't omniscient, so after you engage in planning you must still expect the unexpected. And don't go back to the drawing board; stay at the drawing board. Planning is a continuous process of revising your revised revisions.

134

ARMING YOURSELF FIRST: YOUR ATTITUDES AND STRATEGY

WORK THE NET BEFORE YOU NETWORK

Doing a thing well is often a waste of time.

– Robert Byrne

One reason the World Wide Web is a wonderful thing is because it enables you to think in several dimensions. Specifically, you can simultaneously seek information in these four ways: broadly, deeply, both broadly and deeply, and broadly and deeply over time.

■ Sometimes It Only Takes One Good Idea to Succeed

Your time, your energy, and your openness are the main constraints to discovery. You want to stay loose and flexible. You need to be limber to be open-minded. You need to be thinking that the only thing separating you from massive success in helping your children is discovering a good program that may change their lives for the better. Keep that thought foremost in your mind as your incentive.

Seek ideas to change your ways of thinking—new ways that will shake your old ways up. Recognize that what you're doing is expanding into the universe. Expansion is important right up to the point of contraction. Once you begin networking, you will have begun to narrow. You'll find that people are much better at narrowing their focus than they are at expanding it. Don't narrow before you're ready. Keep your options open as long as you can.

DIG HERE, DIG THERE, BUT DON'T DIG EVERYWHERE

As important as it is to do research, your time is probably limited, so you won't always be able to look in depth. Avoid time wasting by doing only superficial research, focusing

CHAPTER FIVE

exclusively on one program, or getting nothing accomplished by procrastinating. What will consistently yield success is for you to survey the field, eliminate unsuitable options, and then concentrate on a few good ones.

■ An Effective Search Strategy

The lessons here go back to your first dating experiences. If you go steady right out of the gate, you'll never know if you've got a lemon or not. On the other hand, if you only play the field, you'll never go slowly enough to smell the flowers—to experience the joys that only a deeper relationship can bring. Then, if you do nothing, you'll get what you paid for...namely, whatever comes along. Somehow you've got to strike a balance between approaches one and two, in whatever sequence makes sense to you. That is, you need to play the field and eventually go steady. In other words, you must survey the choices, eliminate the obvious lemons, narrow in on the remainder, and then make a commitment.

SURVEY THE FOREST FIRST, THEN THE TREES

> *The trouble with life in the fast lane is that you get to the other end in an awful hurry.*
>
> – John Jensen

Probably the biggest mistake parents make in helping their children find good programs, services, and products is not surveying the field. The main reason parents don't survey, I suspect, is that they can't. Surveying the field is hard to do. It takes lots of time, energy, and commitment—all things that are rarely available to most parents.

136

ARMING YOURSELF FIRST: YOUR ATTITUDES AND STRATEGY

■ Nothing Is as Cost-Effective as a Good Overview

How long would it take you to find a lost dog in a cornfield if you followed his trail on foot, vs. flew around in a helicopter? That's an easy one, isn't it? Having an overview makes sense. When we can have one, we usually do. The problem with having an overview about programs, services, and products for children is that it's very difficult to conduct one. Using the same illustration, we can't all afford helicopters, and without a helicopter an overview is much more difficult. On the other hand, even though it may be more costly or difficult in the near term, getting an overview may be cheaper and easier than the alternatives.

Getting an overview is a form of shorthand, only more so. An overview cuts to the chase, so to speak. It not only enables something to be discovered more quickly, but it also increases the chances for the right choice to be made, avoiding costly errors. Using the example I started with, hunting for a dog on the ground can be very misleading. You may be chasing who knows what else. Having an overview will take care of the problem more easily.

■ An Overview Puts Everything in Perspective

Another way of thinking of an overview is as a way of putting things in perspective. It's very easy to get caught up in the moment and forget the long-range view, because putting out immediate fires usually takes precedence over other things. The long view is important, but it frequently must get bumped. The question is: What gets it back on track?

■ An Overview Puts Everything in Context

Yet another way of thinking of an overview is as a context.

CHAPTER FIVE

It's very easy to forget the context of what you're considering because the view of your context is frequently obscured by any number of phenomena. Again, the issue is what gets you headed back in the right direction.

What can bring you back? To have an overview, keep your perspective, or be persistently aware of your context, you must be in "overview mode," which is a kind of a reserved-judgment posture. This is where you're "keeping your powder dry"— conserving resources for a time when you may really need to deploy them. This is also where you put on your skeptic's hat, strap on your doubter's face, and turn on your cynic's point of view. You might hear yourself say, "Let's hear the benefits," or "I'm from the Show Me State," or "What's the bottom line?" This is a good way to fulfill your overview role.

Parenting is about having an overview role for children who have insufficient information to make good judgments. What we're talking about here is how to parent better by increasing both the effort that is being made at having an overview as well as using better overview tools, which follows from making a greater effort.

■ The Engineer's Credo Should Be Modified

This is all to the good, but it makes for modification of one of the sacred, powerful, and practical models of human life: the engineer's credo, which is that the shortest distance between two points is a straight line. My modification of the engineer's credo is this: The most efficient way from point "A" to point "B" is to take a fly-over first.

And just consider what this implies. Having an overview means that you do have a broader perspective of what direction your children may be heading in. It means you have a

138

ARMING YOURSELF FIRST: YOUR ATTITUDES AND STRATEGY

plan. Think about it. You can't have an overview unless you have something longer-range in mind.

■ Your Most Valuable Job as Parent Is the Overview

Another way of putting this is to say that, if you don't have an overview of your children's lives, you have a problem, Houston, because having an overview is really what parenting is all about. It is the "value proposition" (in investor-speak) that you provide for your children—their reason for having you around. So do your job better. If you have an overview, improve upon it. If you don't have an overview, get one. This is the only way you can stay a few steps ahead of your kids. If you don't stay a few steps ahead of your kids, you may not like the consequences.

SEARCH, NARROW, SELECT, CONNECT, EVALUATE

Searching for, narrowing, selecting, connecting with, and evaluating children's programs, services, and products is not, cannot be, and should not be a neat linear operation where one step clearly follows from the last. However, hypothetically, the process might resemble the diagram shown on page 140, "The Ideal Situation." This is the perfect case . . . the one-in-a-million situation that proceeds too smoothly to be believed.

Reality may actually turn the process into something more like the second diagram, "The More Likely Course." This latter procedure involves a lot more change, wheel spinning, back-pedaling, hovering, and side-to-side motion. But in the end, you'll probably wind up in the same place.

In simple terms, the process resembles going to a restaurant you've never been to before and selecting your order from the menu. Sometimes this is easy. There may be only one

139

CHAPTER FIVE

The Ideal Situation	**The More Likely Course**

The Ideal Situation

Overview (The Search)
↓
Narrowing
↓
Selection
↓
Connection
↓
Evaluation
↻

The More Likely Course

↖ Overview (The Search)
⇄ Overview → Overview ↘
↳ Selection ↓ Pause ↻
↙ Narrowing ↗ Connection
⇈
↖ Connection ↺
∩ Selection ↘
↳ Pause ↘
⇊ Selection ↗
↓↑
↓ Connection ↘
↯
↳ Evaluation
Overview ↲
↻

thing on the menu that appeals to you. Other times this is very difficult, especially when you see many items you might want to select.

However it turns out, what's important is that you, as parent, engage in all the key steps instead of just one or two, so that your children may benefit. A brief description of each of the steps may deliver my point.

■ Overview (Selection)

Scanning the choices is a continuous process of keeping your ears to the ground, your nose to the air, and your eyes on the horizon. Your attitude always reflects your knowledge of your children and the direction they're heading in. Your attitude needs to be open, flexible, skeptical, and discriminating (with

140

ARMING YOURSELF FIRST: YOUR ATTITUDES AND STRATEGY

a smile on your face), as you devise, plan, and formulate again their current and future plans. You need to be constantly thinking next day, next week, next month, and next year. The process of overview (selection) resembles picking up tools for any task. You're attracted to any candidate that looks like it might have the potential of doing the job. It's always wise to choose at first more than you may actually end up using.

■ Narrowing

Trimming, winnowing down, cutting back, and thinning out is always more difficult than scanning and selecting anything that moves, for now you must begin to distinguish what may actually be useful. Your powers of observation and analysis kick in here. You make a supreme effort to differentiate among many similar choices—comparing and contrasting features and benefits while considering the factors and limitations that bear upon your child's future.

■ Selection

Coming down to a few choices is an extension of narrowing, only more challenging. You must focus even more, becoming even more discriminating. This will require more mental energy as you come down to just a few choices.

■ Connection

Attaching, linking up, connecting, and bonding is the final step in the process. Adjustment begins.

■ Evaluation

The matching of expectations with reality is the key process here. At this point, you may be seeing totally different things from what your children see.

CHAPTER FIVE

CIRCLE IT, DON'T MARRY IT

Life is what happens while you're making other plans.

– John Lennon

Surveying the forest means staying somewhat remote from the process so you can witness the broad effects. As the parent, you are the omniscient one. You must keep stepping back and reevaluating your sense of the whole.

Your child and you are a team. Your child sees the program up close and personal, while you see the process more objectively, from afar. Keep it that way until your child can perform both functions.

HOW TO WORK A CHILDREN'S FAIR

There are worse things in life than death. Have you ever spent an evening with an insurance salesman?

– Woody Allen

Working a children's fair (by this I mean an exposition dedicated to the marketing of children's programs, services, and products) is an ideal way to search, narrow, select, connect, and evaluate. By all means attend any children's expo or fair in your area—as long as you do so in a Trojan horse.

Just remember that the people in the booths are not there for their health. They're there to sell, and in this selling mode they will probably not be completely objective. That is to say, they may make a few exaggerated claims, they may knock the competition, and they may patronize you more than you might expect from a normal person who's disinterested in your family's affairs. They certainly won't know your children as you do, nor have their best interests in mind.

142

ARMING YOURSELF FIRST: YOUR ATTITUDES AND STRATEGY

On the other hand, such a fair can be a tremendous benefit to you in time savings and in improving your parenting, not to mention a great benefit to your children if you find programs and services there that make a big difference in your children's upbringing. If you can take advantage of such an opportunity, here are some suggestions about how to work a fair.

■ Have a Plan

Go there with a plan in mind, or at least a few focused questions. Whether you wind up abandoning this plan or modifying it, having a plan will help you organize your time and focus your energies. What is a plan? It can be any number of things: an idea to put your children in an after-school or summer program; a notion about solving a medical issue, such as a speech impediment; or an idea about getting your child involved on the road to participation in the Olympics.

Whatever it may be, begin with an end in mind. You should have some ideas about what your children's strengths and weaknesses are. If you have no ideas at the moment, think about this. You may find programs to overcome a weakness or services to build upon strengths. A few examples for building on strengths are: Is your child a Mozart in disguise? Is she a Tiger Woods clone? Can he be a world class juggler in his spare time? A few examples for overcoming weaknesses are: Would you like to help your child get over being so shy? Are there alternatives to the use of drugs for hyperactivity? If you're a single parent, can you find help for dealing with adjustment issues?

The childhood issues along these lines could fill volumes, so a small amount of focus will probably flood your mind

143

CHAPTER FIVE

with ideas. A longer-range setup plan can also work here: How can I plan ahead to get my child into the best high school or college? What are several realistic development alternatives for my child becoming an entertainer? What are the pros and cons of home schooling?

■ Play the Field

Play the field, at least to begin. Let's say you've come to the fair with a plan. This is good. You're directed. You now have a road map to getting some questions answered. But before you go too far too fast, here's some friendly advice: When you get to the fair, guard against getting too specific too fast. Survey what's there first. Walk around. Get familiar with the categories that the programs, services, and products fall into. Walk completely around the fair before you stop at a single booth, checking out all the rows, all the isles, all the conference rooms, and all the directories. Read the program, if one was handed to you.

Sound kind of silly? Perhaps. But here's the benefit: staying focused. The fair is a smorgasbord of programs, services, and products of all kinds. It's very easy to get distracted, and in the process wear yourself out before you reach your objectives. This is similar to going to the supermarket. You can go to a market and put whatever catches your eye on impulse into your shopping cart. You can also go there very focused on eggs and milk. There are benefits to both approaches, but generally, if time is an issue for you, it will benefit you more to stay focused. Surveying the entire layout will enable you to find and prioritize the top three places you need to visit. It will also keep your mind open to choices you never thought about that may better meet your needs.

144

ARMING YOURSELF FIRST: YOUR ATTITUDES AND STRATEGY

■ Read Labels Carefully

Assuming you've come to the fair with a plan in mind and you've completed your initial survey, you're now ready to go to the few booths you've targeted. You'll be doing some comparison shopping.

Remember that the built-in bias of the participants is selling. They're going to focus mainly on positive benefits. They won't tell you what they've left out of the picture. Divide your time among the few providers that interest you. Review your plan, then dive in. Introduce yourself. Present your questions. Take notes if you can. Collect everything you can, then go on to the next provider.

Do the same with all the remaining providers, until you've completed talking with each of them at least once. Once you've collected everything, go home and create a file. Use whatever method works best for you; for example, put everything in a loose-leaf binder. Next, create a small spreadsheet (by hand or on computer) of the key features of each plan. This need not be elaborate.

If you have time to do comparison reading and study before the fair is over, go back and ask another round of questions. Factor in to the questions you ask now the unique characteristics of your children. The finer points will begin to appear after your first review, such as omissions of information that weren't obvious before.

If you have time for a third go-around, do it. You should go back as many times as you need to, to clarify issues. When you go back, resist the temptation to decide there and then which one to choose. No doubt you will be asked; this is just good salesmanship at work.

145

CHAPTER FIVE

■ Three . . . Three's Good

How many program candidates should you select? After all there are hundreds of children's programs, services, and products and perhaps quite a large number of those that may work well for your children. There are a number of good answers to this question. For example, find as many programs as you have time to do the research for; or keep looking until you have a good feeling about what you've found (or at least a minimum of bad feelings); or look until you've found at least two you just have to have and can't decide between. There is no right answer here. If one of the answers just cited doesn't appeal, then just try three programs. Three is not a round number. Three is not especially a significant number. There's nothing magical about three. Three's a good number, however, when you haven't found any other reason to stop looking.

■ Eliminate, Then Negotiate

Inevitably you'll be leaning toward one or another of the providers. Yet each of the provider programs under consideration will probably have features that you like. It probably won't be possible to get all the features you want in a single program, service, or product. So, at this point, ask yourself *Who would I rather have if I could get anyone?* If you can't decide among the providers, keep studying or spend more time with them, just getting to know them and their organizations.

When you've made a choice, go back to the provider you've chosen and ask questions in such a manner that you let it be known you'll select their program if they'll just provide something (within reason) that' s missing that the other

146

ARMING YOURSELF FIRST: YOUR ATTITUDES AND STRATEGY

provider is offering. This is negotiation time. You may not get what's missing offered to you, but you may get something else of equal or greater value. It's also important that you clarify your expectations in this process so that they're realistic and as clear as possible. It's not fair to the program or to your children to inflate your expectations.

■ Get Down and Assess

Signing up and paying for a program you've reviewed but never experienced shouldn't be done on a long-term basis. Choose the shortest trial period you can. It may be more expensive in the short run to do this, as many programs offer discounts for long-term signups. However, the missed discounts will be "money well spent" compared to what it might cost to undo a mistaken selection.

Many things in life, including children's programs, can't be fairly evaluated until you actually get involved with them. There are just too many unknowns, the biggest ones being your children's responses to the instructor, the other children, and the surroundings. There may be nothing wrong with the program, but your children's interest may not be very high, simply because it isn't the right fit for them.

If you can, give every new program a trial period, then evaluate the results using the plan you had in mind, to compare performance with your expectations. Evaluating what's happening is the only way to continually make improvements to what's going on in the program and with your children. Don't skip this important step, for it will lead to the next program, service, or product that you select, at a later time, for your children.

147

CHAPTER FIVE

YOU MUST HAVE AN ATTITUDE

If you aren't fired with enthusiasm, you will be fired with enthusiasm.

– Vince Lombardi

Engaging in challenging tasks calls for a significant amount of mental preparation. If you don't already know that successful child rearing is a stiff challenge, you're probably not involved in parenting yet. Mental preparation means acquiring the right frame of mind for the task. Some people call this attitude. It might be thought of as armor, because it's partly defensive. Others might term it assertive programming, because it's also proactive. Ideally, good parenting is second nature. This is a state in which you're pushing forward with minimal exertion because you're so well prepared for what can and does occur. Here you can respond positively in most situations, with clarity and consistency. More realistically, most parenting will be heavily taxing because so much of it is done spur of the moment in on-the-job training.

■ Give a Little, Ask a Lot

When selecting children's programs, services, and products, having an attitude is an important part of having a good overall parental attitude. The attitude will lead to healthy questions to ask yourself, your children, and your providers, to evaluate how well their offerings fit your children's needs. Having an attitude means coming to the party with some ideas in mind about how things work.

Here are the components of an attitude that's most favorable to getting the selection job done well:

148

ARMING YOURSELF FIRST: YOUR ATTITUDES AND STRATEGY

✦ *There is much more than meets the eye.* It's up to you, as parent, to uncover the hidden parts of children's programs, services, and products. Keep digging until you run out of time. How do you dig? Ask a lot of questions. Asking good questions demands a good imagination, and both foresight and hindsight.

✦ *The information offered by children's providers is probably inadequate, misleading, or not clearly communicative.* You must delve beneath the surface and question everything written down.

✦ *When in doubt, ask general, open-ended questions.* Specific questions may be too threatening and may generate misleading answers, i.e., defensive responses. Examples of open-ended questions are: "So, tell me about your program," or "Will children enjoy the program?"

✦ *Program providers are selecting you as much as you're selecting them.* Learning is a two-way street. Providers have a profile of their ideal candidate just as you do. If, instead of shopping around any further, you know that you want your child to be accepted into a certain program, you must sell them on the idea that your child meets their profile. The way to sell them on your child is by asking questions instead of making declarations. If you must make a declaration, sometimes assuming the negative will elicit the positive. "My son may not be a good candidate for your program because he . . ." might be a good opening to generate an argument in your son's favor. Also, if you lead with an assumption, they may correct you.

149

CHAPTER FIVE

+ *When in doubt, decide in favor of your children.* Don't select something only because you would have liked it for yourself and never had it; don't select something because you met a nice person; and don't select something because one of your friends did. Remember why you went to the fair, and leave fulfilling the plan you had in mind when you arrived. In fact, one of your best reasons for making your plan beforehand was so you wouldn't make a decision for any other reason than that it was good for your children.

+ *If your children are along, ask them if they have any questions about programs you encounter.* Don't ask them leading questions (directing them to an answer they think you want to hear), loaded questions (ones you already know the answers to), or coaxing questions (that persuade them not so subtly that this is your preferred choice). Genuinely ask their opinion with an open-ended (any answer is okay) type of question. Then listen for their response. You may be surprised at how perceptive they are.

UNFORTUNATELY, YOU CAN'T BE FIRED

The worst thing about being a parent is that you can't be fired for incompetence unless your shortcomings are incredibly blatant. Being just mediocre at parenting doesn't merit a short-term penalty of any kind.

And that's the good news. The bad news is the long run. Your kids will become a kind of living scorecard of your efforts. They'll reap the benefits of your successes and pay the ultimate price, if there is a price to pay, for your failures. Of course, you'll share in this payment or reward too.

Come to think of it, it might be good if parents could be

150

ARMING YOURSELF FIRST: YOUR ATTITUDES AND STRATEGY

fired for incompetence. Such a fate might spare us from seeing the results of our poor work unfold before our eyes for the rest of our lives!

■ Bite the Bullet and Accept the Blame

The best policy to adopt is that the buck stops with you, whether or not this is absolutely true. No matter what happens, you're mainly responsible anyway. You know this. This is not a mystery. First of all, your children are your genes personified. Your family history guides their future. Second, your children are in your orbit. You are their mentor in all your behavior, positive and negative. Third, you have the power of life and death over them. This is an awesome responsibility and one not to be taken too lightly. Your children sit at your feet and await your leadership, which doesn't mean dictatorship but guidance based upon insight, foresight, and due diligence.

THERE'S NO THERE, THERE — OR, WHERE ARE THE EMPEROR'S CLOTHES?

As parent, you're a leader, you're responsible, and you're expected to be omniscient. You've already had your childhood and your opportunities to prepare for being a good parent. It's show time now.

One of the hardest jobs a parent has is seeing or foreseeing what's not there. Specifically, when you're hunting for children's programs, services, and products, what you can't immediately see is often what's critical to the success of the program. The question is, how do you see what isn't visible? How can you tell what's not been told to you? How can you sense what's missing from the information presented to you?

151

CHAPTER FIVE

■ Noticing What's Missing

It sometimes takes courage to be the first to notice something missing and ask about it. Sometimes it's not courage that's required so much as your powers of observation. Then again, it may be your memory that's being tested. The only other useful method of noticing what's not obvious is to carefully compare what's on a written listing to what you see before your eyes.

■ Some Things Preclude Others

Some programs, services, and products for children are one thing because they are not another. For example, a piano class might be very flexible for different schedules because it isn't taught by anyone special. A child may have a good eye for color because she has no talent for math. A teacher is wonderful at writing because he can't communicate verbally.

■ Some Things Include Others

Other times, children's programs, services, and products are both one thing and another. For example, a juggling class is both fun and developmentally rich because it depends upon students mastering eye-hand coordination skills. Or a swimming class offers not only a valuable skill to learn for emergencies but also a good technique for keeping in shape. Or learning to dance not only applies musical talent but results in positive social interaction as well.

■ Some Things Are the Sum Total of Everything

At other times, a program, service, or product is what it is because it's the sum total of all the known and unknown factors present. For example, good progress made in a drawing

152

ARMING YOURSELF FIRST: YOUR ATTITUDES AND STRATEGY

class may result from the talent and effort brought to the class by the student, the instruction skill brought to the table by the instructor, the nature of the assignments given, and the specific drawing medium selected. A sailing class success might result from an interaction among all the elements, favorable and unfavorable, that come to the sea that day.

■ Noticing Omissions Means Using All Your Parental Faculties

It takes energy, focus, courage, memory, experience, observation, creativity, and mechanical effort to see what's not there. This is a very important parenting skill. Parents have to dig deeper than normal to be good at it. In addition, parents must realize that it's both what we do and what we don't do that counts. That is to say, not doing is doing.

Always beware of what's not there, because it can be more important than what *is* there. The negative is at least as important as the positive when it comes to influences in your children's lives.

A SUMMARY OF CHAPTER FIVE

Your child is completely unique from everyone who has ever been, so the odds are stacked against his excelling in a typical school, one that targets a norm few fit into. Relax about this, give your child a break, and respect his uniqueness. Search for programs, services, and products that will assist you in enhancing his development or resolving any real problems.

Your child will build his character from the traits he learns by observing you or your parental substitutes over the long term. He will learn skills through enrollment with skill-mentoring specialists in and out of school. Seeking, connecting,

CHAPTER FIVE

and evaluating programs, services, and products is most efficiently done with special problem-solving skills, a plan in mind, a proactive attitude, and careful overview skills that can be acquired with awareness, insight, and practice.

ASSIGNMENT FOR CHAPTER FIVE

Say you have a family of four children and your youngest child stutters. Diagnose what the cause of this might be and come up with a plan to enhance your little one's development and build her skills. By describing a strategy to suit her needs, select a series of programs, services, and products that might help her.

CHAPTER 6

Preparing for Takeoff

I have a simple philosophy. Fill what's empty. Empty what's full. Scratch where it itches.

– Alice Roosevelt Longworth

You're now ready to begin making preparations to take off— armed with foresight, insight, and attitude. What you may need now, to be completely prepared, is a few handy, last-minute tools to use on your journey.

MAYBE YOU'RE STILL NOT SURE

How and what to choose? You've been thinking about that for the last few chapters, so you know how to do all that now. What you may not have thought about yet is how to sift through all the choices to make your ultimate selections. Here's a suggestion: organize what you've found into broad categorical heaps, stacks, or piles and give them names that make sense to you.

This will be at least a four-step process on your part:

1. Gather together your information on some *programs* such as after-school programs.

2. Invent general *categories* for the programs you've found, such as creative programs.

155

CHAPTER SIX

3. *Sort* the programs into the categories you've invented *using one particular objective*, such as taking a dance class after school.

4. *Reorganize*, if necessary, by starting over, finding more programs, inventing more categories, and doing more sorting under a different objective, such as looking for other after-school eye-hand coordination activities.

PROGRAMS, PROGRAMS, PROGRAMS

To reiterate, the word "programs" as I'm using it is a loose description of all the different activities, services, and products offered by various providers to children in your community. They can be public or private, for-profit or nonprofit, large-scale or small-scale, serious or fun. They can include after-school programs, flute lessons, square dancing classes, speech therapy, learning to swim, toys to play with, archery practice, water slides, rock climbing, face painting, ballet, sailing, Special Olympics, and many, many other possibilities.

■ Program Categories

Here's a suggested list of program categories for you to use.

✦ Programs for the fun of it: (examples: programs you just want your children to have fun in, such as wind surfing, fishing)

✦ Programs for survival (examples: health, medical, or nutritional programs)

✦ Programs to build on (examples: skill enhancement programs such as sailing, yo-yoing, juggling, kite flying)

PREPARING FOR TAKEOFF

+ Programs for independence (examples: reading club, scouting, fixing things, religious training)

+ Programs for building social skills (examples: ballroom dance class, group sports, parties)

+ Programs for free play (examples: sand castle building, playground visits)

+ These programs aren't for sale (examples: free counseling advice, free programs for children at museums)

+ Default programs (examples: physical education and other routine school programs)

+ Programs for problems (examples, programs to address drugs or teen pregnancy)

+ Programs for the creative (examples: singing, sewing, fine arts, robot building)

Categories that pop into your mind and leap onto the page may have a lot to do with the particular needs your children have. Why? Because you're a parent, and parents know about these things. What are those needs? Well they might be skills your children don't have and need to acquire, bad habits they practice too much and need to break, or problems they have that need fixing. You'll know what these are. Try listing them on paper and making them into categories, instead of just fretting about them.

Don't forget to get your kids involved in this exercise, too. Remember that each of your children will have a completely unique set of programs and categories, applicable only to them.

CHAPTER SIX

■ Sorting by One Set of Rules

Going back to our discussion on problem solving in Chapter Four, sorting is important because it is a method of slicing problems in a certain way. If you look at your child's problem behavior as a symptom of some other problem instead of a problem in and of itself, that's sorting the problem one way. If, on the other hand, you look at your child's problem behavior as the problem, instead of a symptom, then that's sorting it a different way.

What does sorting according to one set of rules mean? To answer that, we must first agree on what is meant by rules. Well, the rules of this first exercise might be: You can list any program under any group, as long as the program is not in more than one group at one time.

Let's take just one category as an example: programs for the fun of it. You might choose to put yo-yoing, clowning, and juggling in that category—activities that your children can engage in just to have fun. You could have put these particular programs in other categories you've invented as well, such as programs to develop eye-hand coordination or programs that kids can call their own or programs that use skill toys. However, you've decided that putting them in the category of programs for the fun of it made sense because your kids really don't want to get much more out of them than just having a ball. They aren't interested in becoming champions or making it serious.

Got the idea? Now sort your programs into categories that address purposes you're trying to accomplish.

■ Reorganizing

Reorganizing, as I'm using the word, simply means to sit

158

back and think of your child's problems, skill needs, and challenges in a different way. Thinking of problems in more than one way often results in better problem solving. The whole idea of this entire exercise is to get you to think about programs in ways you haven't done before. Why? Because there is usually a lot more contained in any program than meets the eye. Our simple human minds frequently trap us into certain channels of thought because we instinctively try to simplify all that comes to mind, perhaps in order to remember things better. This is not a good thing to do with children's programs when you're in the selection mode. Seemingly simple programs may have profound lessons to teach our children if we will just look at them with a more open mind. So reorganize to your heart's content. Every time you do, you'll gain another insight and make the selection of a valuable set of programs a lot easier.

■ Walk Around on Paper

Noting things down on paper and visualizing things in your mind is much easier than doing real walking, or even letting your fingers do the walking. The visualization and notation process burns only a few calories, but may save you a lot of time, energy, and money. Writing things down on paper is a very efficient method of organizing your thoughts. Try it, if you don't already use it. It works.

BE A BALANCING ARTIST

In creating categories, remember the importance of maintaining a balance in your children's lives. Balance can mean any number of things. Here it means putting together a satisfying and harmonious array of activities and a level of engagement

CHAPTER SIX

that fulfills your children's needs, so that nothing is unduly emphasized at the expense of the whole. You know that your children need many skills to succeed in life, and that early exposure will give them an edge that will help them have a good and rewarding life.

What are your children's needs? That's not an easy question to answer; however, the implicit philosophies working here are that (1) too much of anything is not a good thing and (2) not enough of some things isn't good either. So exposure to a wide array of programs is desirable at the same time that concentration on just a few is. This is a riddle that only a balancing artist such as a parent can address. Since this balance is different for everyone, the concept of balance is difficult to define specifically for anyone. A sustained effort at trial and error will probably be the only way to discover the ideal balance for your children. I've heard it said that we're never in balance. If that's true, then probably balance is what we should always be striving for, though it may always be a fluid thing.

An example of the need for balance might be that, for whatever reason, you have enrolled your son in sporting activities only: ice hockey, soccer, baseball, football, track and field games, swimming, surfing, bowling, volleyball, gymnastics, wrestling, and golf. Let's assume that this is an extreme example of being out of balance because there are so many sports activities. The question is what effect this will have on your son in the long run. Will he become addicted to sports to the exclusion of all other activities life has to offer (art, reading, music, plays)? Will he hate sports because he got too much of them? Will he only be able to relate to people of like experiences?

Similarly, what if your daughter spent all her time on solo computer activities? Would she become a social outcast because she had learned so few social skills as a result of spending so much time alone?

Before we leave the subject of balance, one final word of advice: Do encourage both your boys and your girls to play with dolls. This is one of the few remaining ways to learn good parenting skills. In playing with dolls, your children will be practicing their parenting skills by mimicking the excellent way that you parent them. Boys—more than ever—need to learn to parent too, so don't deprive them of this important skill.

A SUMMARY OF CHAPTER SIX

Sorting, organizing, and reorganizing is a method of thinking on paper how best to select from among all the potential choices you have in developing your child. It's an analysis technique whose purpose is to enlighten you as rapidly as possible, open your mind to different possibilities, and remove artificial boundaries where they may exist—such as any preconceptions you may have inadvertently brought to the table. Remember that it's quicker and cheaper to discover things on paper than in reality. Use this technique until you've exhausted its usefulness.

ASSIGNMENT FOR CHAPTER SIX

Imagine that your child was born with a deformed leg that inhibits her from participating in some of the active sports children commonly participate in. First, think of some programs that will enhance her childhood development. Next, think of categories of programs that may be related to her de-

CHAPTER SIX

velopment. Next, sort the programs you've thought of into the categories you've selected. Then reorganize the initial sorting at least two more times, to get a different perspective on what may better help. Finally, instead of just trying to resolve certain issues your child may have, create a balanced program that will help her resolve some obvious difficulties she'll face and at the same time help her develop herself for a rich and fulfilling life ahead.

CHAPTER 7

Now Zero In

If it weren't for the last minute, nothing would get done.

– Unknown

Eventually, all your efforts must come to a conclusion, comfortably or not. Although this book is presented as a series of hypothetical exercises, in your busy life you won't have much of a choice when you've run out of time to plan for your children, so you want to get everything accomplished while you can. Be content. This is a happy situation. Making decisions enable us to go on with our lives. We won't be stuck in a permanent rut.

INVOLVE YOUR CHILDREN

Should you make all the decisions? Sure, if you want your kids to be dependent upon you for the rest of their lives. You'll also be giving yourself a lot of extra work that way. But go ahead. It'll be a lot quicker and less frustrating—in the short run. Go ahead and get it over with, chump. Be a control freak, if you must.

If you want some good advice, though, do yourself a big favor and don't do this. Involve your children every step of the way, even if they're very young and seemingly have little understanding of the omniscient picture. Give them friendly

CHAPTER SEVEN

nudges when they get stuck. Joke with them. Help them laugh in the process.

Should you go to the other extreme and leave it all up to them? Nope. You should all be involved. You need to be giving them pointers about the consequences of obviously harmful choices.

Should you all close your eyes and just choose? No, not if you all haven't answered any of the important questions that lead up to a choice. Yes, if you've all already boiled down the choices to just a few. If you make the wrong choice after a lot of work, you can always go back and choose again without much risk of loss.

ULTIMATELY, IT'S THEIR DECISION

All the sections of this book have been leading up to this point, and we've come down to my last piece of advice: Don't dictate your solution. Instead, help facilitate your children's decision on the programs, services, and products in which they'll get involved. Let them in on some good strategies to follow, such as the reasoning behind your putting programs in certain categories. Instead of giving them only one category to think about, select three categories, and then ask them to choose one. Accompany that choice with a lot of caveats and contingency plans.

Let's add a few pointers to that sage advice, for good measure.

WHAT WILL A GOOD CLOSURE LOOK LIKE?

It'll be full of caveats (qualifications) and contingencies (alternatives in case things don't work out). It's all going to boil down to a few sentences in your head, or maybe on paper

164

NOW ZERO IN

if you want to keep your mind free and clear for other things. In fact, I recommend this, because when you put pen to paper, magic occurs.

It might look something like this:

Well okay, we'll choose _____
(this program) first, and see what happens. We're choosing this program because _____.
If everything goes right and _____
happens, then we'll follow it up with _____
_____ (this program).
If the unexpected happens and makes _____
happen, we'll proceed with _____.
If all else fails, then we'll employ _____
_____ as a backup plan.

How often shall you do this? As often as it is useful, which I hope I've persuaded you will be frequently.

WHAT WILL A GOOD CLOSURE FEEL LIKE?

A child becomes an adult when he realizes that he has a right not only to be right but also to be wrong.

– Thomas Szasz

Well, it certainly won't feel complete. There'll still be many questions and loose ends left outstanding about the programs you've selected, such as what if your child doesn't like it.

Selecting programs for your children is time-consuming, sometimes frustrating, and seemingly endless, while they're still children. But one day they'll be grown and your responsibilities will suddenly come to an end. At that time, if you've done your parenting job well, you will have taught your

165

CHAPTER SEVEN

children to select well for themselves without your assistance, because you've gone through this process many times with them instead of soloing by yourself.

If you have allowed them to participate in this process with you, they will not only have made good choices, but they will also have learned valuable life lessons from you.

I hope that, in the long process you will have shared with your children, you'll have let them make their own mistakes, giving them the opportunity to experience failure when the stakes are still low and easy to recover from.

WHAT IF THE WHOLE PROCESS FAILS?

It won't, but if you think it might, reread some of these chapters. Rethink your plan. Make some different choices. Start halfway to the end of your plan and make changes. Keep the first half. If that fails, discard the first half and redesign it.

If you've read this book, you've got a good start. Many other resources are available to consult; I've listed some of them in the appendices that follow. Do more homework. This is always good advice, because life offers so much to know and so little time. And remember: Even though the decision-making years will eventually reach their end, parenting is for life. It will never be over. (And then there's grandparenting . . .)

SUMMARY OF CHAPTER SEVEN

All good things must come to an end, and every ending is just the beginning of another great adventure. Deciding on one approach after having looked at many is a necessary and very agreeable step. It isn't cast in stone, but if done right it's very rewarding. You've done all you could and now it's time to test your findings, insights, and conclusions.

NOW ZERO IN

ASSIGNMENT FOR CHAPTER SEVEN

Using the results of the assignment at the end of Chapter Six, lay out in one sentence a single conclusion that describes the choice made by you and your child, some alternatives to that choice, all caveats and contingencies you can think of, and your backup plan.

APPENDIX 1

Helpful Guides

Books: A tremendous number of publications on children's affairs are available. My check of Amazon.com found the following sheer numbers: Children's Life — 10,134; Child Development — 4,843; Children's Services — 2,931; Children's Programs — 1,241; Children's Products — 63; Planning for Children — 243; Child Enrichment — 14; and Scholarships — 518; Besides those, there were 23,150 citations for children's books and 1,275 entries for children's software. There is duplication in these lists, yet they do show the wealth of available resources to help parents address a wide array of childhood issues.

The following is a compilation and sorting of a few of the books found at Amazon as well as others currently available in retail and other online bookstores.

BOOKS ON TOYS

Auerbach, Stevanne, Ph.D. *Dr. Toy's Smart Play*, 1998, St. Martin's Griffin, New York.

Auerbach, Stevanne, and Ben Asen. *Toys for a Lifetime: Enhancing Childhood Through Play*, 1999, Universe Publishing.

Miller, Joan E. Heller, and Sue Schwartz, Ph.D. *The New Language of Toys: Teaching Communication Skills to Children With Special Needs: A Guide for Parents and Teachers*, 1996, Woodbine House.

Oppenheim, Stephanie, James Oppenheim, and Joanne F. Oppenheim. *Oppenheim Toy Portfolio: 2002 Edition The Best Toys, Books, Videos, Music & Software for Kids*, 2001, Oppenheim Toy Portfolio, Inc.

A BOOK ON ENRICHMENT

Hawkins, Robert P. *School and Home Enrichment Program for Severely Handicapped Children*, 1983, Research Press.

HELPFUL GUIDES

BOOKS ON PLAY

Heidemann, Sandra, et al. *Pathways to Play: Developing Play Skills in Young Children*, 1992, Redleaf Press.

Katch, Jane, and Vivian Gussin. *Under Deadman's Skin: Discovering the Meaning of Children's Violent Play*, 2001, Beacon Press.

Silby, Caroline, Ph.D., and Shelley Smith. *Games Girls Play: Understanding and Guiding Young Female Athletes*, 2000, St. Martin's Press.

BOOKS ON PARENTING

Bennett, Steven J., and Ruth Bennett. *TV-Free Activities You Do With Your Child*, 1996, Adams Media Corporation.

Britton, Lesley, and Joy Starrey Turner. *Montessori Play & Learn: A Parent's Guide to Purposeful Play from Two to Six*, 1993, Crown Publishing.

Cassidy, Anne. *Parents Who Think Too Much: Why We do It, How to Stop It*, 1998, Dell Island Books.

Cline, Foster, M.D., & Jim Fay. *Parenting Teens With Love & Logic: Preparing Adolescents for Responsible Adulthood*, 1993, Navpress.

Cline, Foster, M.D., & Jim Fay. *Parenting with Love and Logic: Teaching Children Responsibility*, 1990, NavPress.

Cox, Meg. *The Heart of a Family: Searching America for New Traditions That Fulfill Us*, 1998, Random House.

Faber, Adele, and Elaine Mazlish. *Siblings Without Rivalry: How to Help Your Children Live Together So You Can Live Too*, 1998, Avon Books.

Faber, Adele, Elaine Mazlish, and Kimberly Ann Coe. *How to Talk So Kids Will Listen & Listen So Kids Will Talk*, 1999, Avon Books.

Ferrucci, Piero. *What Our Children Teach Us: Lessons in Joy, Love and Awareness*, 2001, iPublish PPC.

Forehand, Rex L., and Nicholas Long. *Parenting the Strong-Willed Child: The Clinically Proven Five-Week Program for Parents of Two-To-Six Year-Olds*, 1996, McGraw Hill.

APPENDIX ONE

Gordon, Dr. Thomas. *Parent Effectiveness Training: The Proven Program for Raising Responsible Children*, 1999, Three Rivers Press.

Heidel, John, and Marion Lyman-Mersereau. *Character Education: Grades 6-12 Year 1*, 1999, Incentive Publications.

Kurcinka, Mary Sheedy. *Raising Your Spirited Child: A Guide for Parents Whose Child is More Intense, Sensitive, Perceptive, Persistent, and Energetic*, 1992, Harper Perennial.

Kurcinka, Mary Sheedy. *Kids, Parents, and Power Struggles: Winning for a Lifetime*, 2000, Quill.

MacKenzie, Robert J. *Setting Limits in the Classroom: How to Move Beyond the Classroom Dance of Discipline*, 1996, Prima Press.

MacKenzie, Robert J. *Setting Limits: How to Raise Responsible, Independent Children by Providing Clear Boundaries*, 1998, Prima Press.

Nelsen, Jane, Lynn Lott, and H. Stephen Glenn. *Positive Discipline A-Z, Revised and Expanded 2nd Edition: From Toddlers to Teens, 1001 Solutions to Everyday Parenting Problems*, 1999, Prima Press.

Pantley, Elizabeth, and William Sears, M.D. *Perfect Parenting: The Dictionary of 1,000 Parenting Tips*, 1998, McGraw Hill.

Phelan, Thomas W., Ph.D., and Glen Ellyn. *1-2-3 Magic: Effective Discipline for Children 2-12*, 1996, Child Management.

Rosemond, John. *John Rosemond's Six-Point Plan for Raising Happy, Healthy Children*, 1989, Andrews McMeel Publishing.

Sears, William, and Martha Sears. *The Discipline Book: Everything you Need to Know to Have a Better-Behaved Child-From Birth to Age Ten*, 1995, Little Brown & Co.

Wyckoff, Jerry, and Barbara Unell. *Discipline Without Shouting or Spanking: Practical Solutions to the Most Common Problems*, 1985, Simon & Schuster.

PARENTING CHILDREN WITH SPECIAL NEEDS

Greenspan, Stanley I., M.D., Serena Weider, Ph.D., and Robin Simon. *The Child With Special Needs: Encouraging Intellectual and Emotional Growth*, 1998, Perseus Press.

HELPFUL GUIDES

Hamaguchi, Patricia McAleer. *Childhood Speech, Language, and Listening Problems: What Every Parent Should Know*, 1995, John Wiley & Sons.

Hughes, Daniel A. *Building the Bonds of Attachment: Awakening Love in Deeply Troubled Children*, 1999, Jason Aronson.

Hughes, Daniel A. *Facilitating Developmental Attachment: The Road to Emotional Recovery and Behavioral Change in Foster and Adopted Children*, 2000, Jason Aronson.

Kranowitz, Carol Stock, and Larry B. Silver. *The Out-Of-Sync Child: Recognizing and Coping With Sensory Integration Dysfunction*, 1998, Perigee.

Lande, Aubrey, et al. *Marvelous Mouth Music: Songs for Speech Therapy and Beyond*, 2000, Belle Curve Records.

Levy, Terry M., Michael Orlans, and Kathryn Brohl. *Attachment, Trauma, and Healing: Understanding and Treating Attachment Disorder in Children and Families*, 1998, Child Welfare League of America.

Martin, Katherine L. *Does My Child Have a Speech Problem?* 1997, Chicago Review Press.

Orr, Catherine. *Mouth Madness: Oral Motor Activities for Children*, 1999, Academic Press.

Sowell, Thomas. *Late-Talking Children*, 1998, Basic Books.

Thomas, Nancy L. *When Love is Not Enough: A Guide to Parenting Children with RAD – Reactive Attachment Disorder*, 1997, Families by Design.

Welch, Martha G., M.D., Mary Ellen Mark, and Niko Tinbergen. *Holding Time: How to Eliminate Conflict, Temper Tantrums, and Sibling Rivalry and Raise Happy, Loving, Successful Children*, 1989, Fireside.

A BOOK ON CHILDHOOD PLANNING

Curtis, Debbie. *Reflecting Children's Lives: A Handbook for Planning Child-Centered Curriculum*, 1996, Redleaf Press.

171

APPENDIX ONE

BOOKS ON CHILDHOOD HEALTH

Betschart, Jean, and Nancy Songer. *It's Time to Learn About Diabetes: A Workbook on Diabetes for Children*, Revised Edition, 1995, John Wiley & Sons.

Brown, Bobbi, Annemarie Iverson, and Brooke Shields. *Bobbi Brown Teenage Beauty: Everything You Need to Look Pretty, Natural, Sexy & Awesome*, 2000, Cliff Street Books.

Gladstar, Rosemary. *Rosemary Gladstar's Herbal Remedies for Children's Health*, 1999, Storey Books.

Gorni, Taro and Armanda Mayer Stinchecum (translator). *Everyone Poops*, 1993, Kane/Miller Book Publishing.

Gravelle, Karen. *The Period Book: Everything You Don't Want to Ask (But Need to Know)*, 1996, Walker & Company.

Haduch, Bill, and Rick Stromoski. *Food Rules! The Stuff You Munch, Its Crunch, Its Punch, and Why You Sometimes Lose Your Lunch*, 2001, Dutton Books.

Harris, Robie H., and Michael Emberley. *It's Perfectly Normal: Changing Bodies, Growing Up, Sex, and Sexual Health*, 1996, Candlewick Press.

Jukes, Mavis, and Debbie Tilley. *Growing Up: Straight Talk About First Bras, First Periods, and Your Changing Body (It's a Girl Thing)*, 1998, Knopf.

Madaras, Lynda, Area Madaras, Simon Sullivan, Jackie Aher, and Martin Anderson. *What's Happening to My Body? Book for Boys: A Growing Up Guide for Parents and Sons*, 3rd Edition, 2000, New Market Press.

Myles, Brenda Smith, and Jack Southwick. *Asperger Syndrome and Difficult Moments: Practical Solutions for Tantrums, Rage and Meltdowns*, 1999, Autism Asperger Publishing Co.

Roan, Sharon L. *Our Daughter's Health*, 2001, Hyperion.

Satter, Ellyn. *How to Get Your Kid to Eat But Not Too Much*, 1987, Bull Pub Company.

Schaefer, Valerie Lee, and Norm Bendell. *The Care and Keeping of You: The Body Book for Girls*, 1998, Pleasant Company Publications.

HELPFUL GUIDES

Stevens, Laura J., and William G. Crook. *12 Effective Ways to Help your ADD/ADHD Child: Drug-Free Alternatives for Attention-Deficit Disorders*, 2001, Avery Penguin Putnam.

BOOKS ON FAMILY COMMUNICATION

Chapman, Gary D., and Ross Campbell. *The Five Love Languages of Children*, 1997, Northfield Publishing.

Coleman, Dr. Paul. *How to Say It to Your Kids*, 2000, Prentice Hall Press.

Covey, Stephen R. *The 7 Habits of Highly Effective Families: Building a Beautiful Family Culture in a Turbulent World*, 1997, Golden Books Publishing Company.

Duke, Marshall P., Elisabeth A. Martin, and Stephen Nowicki, Jr. *Teaching Your Child the Language of Social Success*, 1996, Peachtree Publishers.

Garcia, Joseph W. *Sign with Your Baby: How to Communicate With Infants Before They Can Speak*, 1999, Northlight Communications.

Giler, Janet Z. *Socially ADDept: A Manual for Parents of Children with ADHD and/or Learning Disabilities*, 2000, C.E.S.

Kurnin, Libby, Ph.D. *Communication Skills in Children With Down Syndrome: A Guide for Parents (Topics in Down Syndrome)*, 1994, Woodbine House.

Levy, Ray, Bill O'Hanlon, and Tyler Norris Goode. *Try and Make Me! A Revolutionary Program for Raising Your Defiant Child—Without Losing Your Cool*, 2001, Rodale Press.

Moorman, Chick. *Parent Talk: Words That Empower, Words That Wound*, 1998, Institute for Personal Power.

Pantley, Elizabeth, and William Sears. *Hidden Messages: What Our Words and Actions Are Really Telling Our Children*, 2000, McGraw Hill.

Powell-Hopson, Darlene, and Derek S. Hopson. *Team Spirited Parenting: 8 Essential Principles for Parenting Success*, 2001, John Wiley & Sons.

Rosenfeld, Alvin, M.D., Nicole Wise, and Robert Coles. *The Over-Scheduled Child: Avoiding The Hyper-Parenting Trap*, 2001, Griffin Trade Paperback.

APPENDIX ONE

Schetz, Katherine F., Pamela G. Taylor, and Stuart K. Cassell. *Talking Together: A Parent's Guide to the Development, Enrichment, and Programs of Speech and Language*, 1994, Pocahontas Press.

Trujillo, Micelle L. *Why Can't We Talk? What Teens Would Share If Parents Would Listen*, 2000, Health Communications.

BOOKS ON SINGLE PARENTING

Anderson, Joan. *The Single Mother's Book: A Practical Guide to Managing Your Children, Career, Home, Finances, and Everything Else*, 1990, Peachtree Publishers.

Brott, Armin A. *The Single Father: A Dad's Guide to Parenting Without a Partner (New Father Series)*, 1999, Abbeville Press, Inc.

Brown, Susan B., and Monica Simmons. *365 Positive Strategies for Single Parenting*, 1998, Smyth & Helwys Publishers.

Clapp, Genevieve. *Divorce & New Beginnings: A Complete Guide to Recovery, Solo Parenting, Co-Parenting and Stepfamilies*, 2000, John Wiley & Sons.

Edin, Kathryn, and Laura Lein. *Making Ends Meet: How Single Mothers Survive Welfare and Low-Wage Work*, 1997, Russell Sage Foundation.

Ellison, Sheila. *The Courage to Be a Single Mother: Becoming Whole Again After Divorce*, 2000, Harper San Francisco.

Green, Daryl D. *My Cup Runneth Over: Setting Goals for Single Parents and Working Couples*, 1998, Pmla.

Karst, Patrice. *The Single Mother's Survival Guide*, 2000, Crossing Press.

Klatte, William C. *Live-Away Dads: Staying a Part of Your Children's Lives When They Aren't a Part of Your Home*, 1999, Penguin USA.

Klungness, Leah, and Andrea Engber. *The Complete Single Mother*, 2000, Adams Business Media.

Lamb, Michael E. (Editor). *The Role of Father in Child Development*, 1996, John Wiley & Sons.

Levy, Judith, and Sophie Allport. *My Baby and Me: A Single Parent's Journal for the First Five Years*, 1999, Stewart Tabori & Chang.

HELPFUL GUIDES

Lofas, Jeannette. *Family Rules: Helping Stepfamilies and Single Parents Build Happy Homes*, 1998, Kensington Publishing Company.

Ludtke, Melissa. *On Our Own: Unmarried Motherhood in America*, 1999, University of California Press.

Mattes, Jane. *Single Mothers by Choice: A Guidebook for Single Women Who Are Considering or Have Chosen Motherhood*, 1997, Times Books.

McLanahan, Sara, and Gary Sandefur. *Growing Up with a Single Parent: What Hurts, What Helps*, 2001, Harvard University Press.

Moffett, Jarni. *Do I Have a Daddy? A Story About a Single-Parent Child*, Jeanne Warren Lindsay, 2000, Morning Glory Press.

Nelsen, Jane, Cheryl Erwin, and Carol Delzer. *Positive Discipline for Single Parents: Nurturing, Cooperation, Respect and Joy in Your Single-Parent Family*, 1999, Prima Press.

Noel, Brook, Arthur C. Klein, and Art Klein. *The Single Parent Resource*, 1998, Champion Publishers Ltd.

Ricci, Isolina, Ph.D. *Mom's House, Dad's House: A Complete Guide for Parents Who Are Separated, Divorced, or Remarried*, 1997, Fireside.

Ross, Julia A., Judy Corcoran, and Ross Corcoran. *Joint Custody with a Jerk: Raising a Child with an Uncooperative Ex*, 1996, St. Martin's Press.

Stanley, Jacqueline D. *Unmarried Parents' Rights (Self-Help Law Kit with Forms)*, 1999, Sourcebooks Trade.

Wassil-Grimm, Claudette. *Where's Daddy: How Divorced, Single and Widowed Mothers Can Provide What's Missing When Dad's Missing*, 1995, Penguin, USA.

Winik, Marion. *The Lunch-Box Chronicles: Notes from the Parenting Underground*, 1999, Vintage Books.

BOOKS ON CHILD DEVELOPMENT PROGRAMS

Bredekamp, Sue (Ed), and Carol Copple (Ed). *Developmentally Appropriate Practice in Early Childhood Programs*, 1997, NYEYC (Series) #234.

Gestwicki, Carol. *Developmentally Appropriate Practice: Curriculum and Development in Early Education*, 1998, Delmer Learning.

APPENDIX ONE

Owocki, Gretchen, and Sue Bredekamp. *Literacy Through Play*, 1999, Heinemann.

BOOKS ON UPBRINGING ISSUES

Clinton, Hillary Rodham. *It Takes a Village, and Other Lessons Children Teach Us*, 1996, Simon & Schuster.

Coontz, Stephanie. *The Way We Really Are: Coming to Terms With America's Changing Families*, 1998, Basic Books.

Kozol, Jonathan. *Savage Inequalities: Children in America's Schools*, 1992, Harper Perennial.

Toth, Jennifer. *Orphans of the Living: Stories of America's Children in Foster Care*, 1997, Touchstone Books.

BOOKS ON HOME SCHOOLING

Albert, David H. *And the Skylark Sings with Me: Adventures in Home-schooling and Community-Based Education*, 1999, New Society Publishers.

Colfax, David, and Micki Colfax. *Homeschooling for Excellence*, 1988, Warner Books.

Dobson, Linda (Editor). *The Homeschooling Book of Answers: The 88 Most Important Questions Answered by Homeschooling's Most Respected Voices*, 1998, Prima Press.

Griffith, Mary, and Lisa Cooper. *Homeschooling Handbook* (Revised 2nd Edition), 1999, Prima Press.

Griffith, Mary. *The Unschooling Handbook: How to Use the Whole World As Your Child's Classroom*, 1998, Prima Press.

Holt, John Caldwell. *How Children Learn*, 1995, Perseus Press.

Holt, John Caldwell. *Learning All the Time*, 1990, Perseus Press.

Layne, Marty. *Learning at Home: A Mother's Guide to Homeschooling*, Revised Edition, 2000, Sea Change Publications.

Llewellyn, Grace. *The Teenage Liberation Handbook: How to Quit School and Get a Real Life and Education*, 1998, Lowry House Publishing.

HELPFUL GUIDES

Ransom, Marsha, and John Taylor. *Complete Idiot's Guide to Homeschooling*, 2001, Alpha Books.

Ratner, Susan. *Kandoo Kangaroo Hops Into Homeschool*, 2000, Master Books.

BOOKS ON FINANCIAL ADVICE FOR CHILDREN

Whitcomb, Dr. John E. *Capitate Your Kids: Teaching Your Teens Financial Independence*, 2001, Popcorn Press.

BOOKS ON ADOPTION

Adamec, Christine A. *The Complete Idiot's Guide to Adoption*, 1998, MacMillan Distribution.

Alexander-Roberts, Colleen. *The Essential Adoption Handbook*, 1993, Taylor Publishing.

Beauvais-Godwin, Laura. *The Complete Adoption Book*, 2000, Adams Media Corporation.

Eldridge, Sherrie. *Twenty Things Adopted Kids Wish Their Adoptive Parents Knew*, 1999, Dell Books.

Gilman, Lois. *The Adoption Resource Book*, 1998, Harperreference.

Gilman, Louis. *The Adoption Resource Book*, 1998, Harperreference.

Helding, Cathy, and Foster W. Cline. *Can This Child Be Saved? Solutions for Adoptive and Foster Families*, 1999, World Enterprises LLC.

Hicks, Randall. *Adopting in America: How to Adopt Within One Year*, 1999, SCB Distributors.

Jewett, Claudia L. *Adopting the Older Child*, 1979, Harvard Common Press.

Johnston, Patricia Irwin. *Adopting after Infertility*, 1996, Perspectives Press.

Keck, Gregory C., and Regina M. Kupecky. *Adopting the Hurt Child: Hope for Families With Special-Needs Kids: A Guide for Parents and Professionals*, 1998, Pinon Press.

177

APPENDIX ONE

Martin, Cynthia D., and Dru Martin Groves. *Beating the Adoption Odds: Using Your Head and Your Heart to Adopt*, 1998, Harvest Books.

Maskew, Trish. *Our Own: Adopting and Parenting the Older Child*, 1999, Snowcap Press.

Melina, Louis Ruskai. *Raising Adopted Children: Practical Reassuring Advice for Every Adoptive Parent*, 1998, Harper Perennial.

Nelson-Erichsen, Jean. *How to Adopt Internationally, 2000-2002 Edition: A Guide for Agency-Directed and Independent Adoptions*, 2000, Mesa House Publishing.

Pertman, Adam. *Adoption Nation: How the Adoption Revolution Is Transforming America*, 2000, Basic Books.

Register, Cherie. *Are Those Kids Yours? American Families With Children Adopted from Other Countries*, 1990, Free Press.

Robinson, Grace. *Older Child Adoption*, 1998, Crossroad/Herder & Herder.

Van Gulden, Holly, and Lisa M. Bartels-Rabb. *Real Parents, Real Children: Parenting the Adopted Child*, 1995, Crossroad/Herder & Herder.

Varon, Lee. *Adopting on Your Own: The Complete Guide to Adoption for Single Parents*, 2000, Farrar Straus & Giroux.

Wallmark, Laurie S. *Adopting: The Tapestry Guide*, 1997, Tapestry Books.

Watkins, Mary, and Susan Fisher. *Talking with Young Children about Adoption*, 1995, Yale University Press.

APPENDIX 2

A Checklist of Children's Programs, Services, and Products

Adventure/Theme Parks

Arts and Crafts
 Dance
 Drawing, Painting, Sculpture
 Music
 Theatre
 Other

Books
 Education
 Leisure

Charities
 Recreation Programs
 Programs for Serious Problem
 Shelters

Clothing

Computers

Educational and Academic
 After-School Programs
 Home Schooling
 Language
 Learning Disabilities
 Private Schools
 Public Schools
 Religious
 Sex Education

Supplemental reading,
 writing, math

Events
 Expos/Fairs
 Pageants
 Shows

Foods
 Restaurants
 Nutrition

Furnishings
 Indoor
 Outdoor

Health
 Preventative

Investments/Lending
 Banking Institutions
 Programs

Learning Disabilities

Legal
 Adoption
 Child Abuse
 Foster Care
 Probation
 Rehabilitation

179

APPENDIX TWO

Leisure Programs

Media/Publications
    Radio/TV/Internet
    Print
    Other

Medical
    Dentistry, Orthodonics,
        Periodontics
    Pediatrics
    Preventative Medicine
    Optometrists, Ophthal-
        mologists
    Naturopathic Medicine
    Specialists: Dyslexia,
        ADHD, Deafness,
        Blindness, Speech
        Defects

Nutrition Programs

Organizations
    Clubs
    Groups

Parents
    Counseling
    Parenting Programs
    Seminars

Parties
    Amusements
    Entertainers
    Party Planners
    Suppliers

Photography

Physical Handicaps

School Programs

School Supplies

Services
    Baby-sitters
    Massage
    Nannies and Au Pairs

Skill Programs

Social
    Adoptions
    Child Care
    Foster Care
    Homeless Care
    Learning-Disadvantaged
    Youth Centers

Sports
    Athletic Team Competi-
        tion
    Individual Sports
    Leisure Programs
    Recreation Programs

Summer
    Activities
    Camp
    Fun
    School

Toys
    Education-based
    Fun-based
    Skill-based
    Sports-related

Travel

Bibliography

Arnold, Johann Christoph. *Endangered: Your Child in a Hostile World*, 2000, Plough Publishing House.

Breeding, John. *The Wildest Colts Make the Best Horses*, 1997, Bright Books.

Breggin, Peter R., and Ginger Ross Breggin. *The War Against Children of Color: Psychiatry Targets Inner-City Youth*, 1998, Common Courage Press.

Byrne, Robert. *1911 Best Things Anybody Ever Said*, 1988, Fawcett Columbine.

Angier, N. "The Purpose of Playful Frolics: Training for Adulthood," *New York Times*, October 20, 1992, pp. C1, C8.

Brosterman, N. *Inventing Kindergarten: Nineteenth Century Children*, 1997, Abrams.

Buhler, C. *From Birth to Maturity: An Outline of the Psychological Development of the Child*, 1935, Kegan Paul.

Caplan, Frank and Theresa. *The Power of Play*, 1973, Anchor Press/ Doubleday.

Cosby, Bill. *Fatherhood*, 1986, Berkley Books.

Crittenden, Ann. *The Price of Motherhood: Why the Most Important Job in the World Is Still the Least Valued*, 2001, Metropolitan Books, Henry Holt & Company.

D'Arcangelo, M. "The Brains Behind the Brain," *Educational Leadership*, 1998, (56)3, 20-25.

Diamond, M., and J. Hopson. *Magic Trees of the Mind: How to Nurture your Child's Intelligence, Creativity and Healthy Emotions from Birth through Adolescence*, 1998, Dutton.

THE PRIVILEGE OF PARENTING

Diller, M.D., Lawrence H. *Should I Medicate My Child? Sane Solutions for Troubled Kids With & Without Psychiatric Drugs*, New York: Basic Books, p.9, 2002.

Duffy, Cathy. *Government Nannies*, 1995, Noble Publishing Associates.

Freud, Sigmund. *Beyond the Pleasure Principle*, in Complete Works, Vol. 18, 1955, Hogarth Press.

Garvey, Catherine. *Play* (in the Developing Child Series), 1990, Harvard University Press.

Hamasaki, Sachio. "Mothering, Fathering and Othering in Kumamoto," in *PlayRights*, Vol. 23, No. 3, p.25-26, Sept. 2001.

Healy, J. *Failure to Connect: How Computers Affect Our Children's Minds—For Better or Worse*, 1998, Simon and Schuster.

Hillman, James. *The Soul's Code: In Search of Character and Calling*, 1996, Random House.

Hull, C. L. *Principles of Behavior*, 1943, Appleton-Century-Crofts.

International Narcotics Control Board (INCB) for 1999 (Report of the). Presented to the United Nations, New York, 2000.

Jambor, T. "Informal, Real-Life Play—Building Children's Brain Connections," *Dimensions of Early Childhood*, 2000, Fall.

Koffka, K. *The Growth of the Mind*, 1946, Kegan Paul.

Lino, Mark. "Expenditures on Children by Families: 1999 Annual Report." U.S.D.A. Center for Nutrition Policy.

McPhee, John. *The Control of Nature*, 1989, Farrar Straus Giroux.

Merrow Report, The (John). *Attention Deficit Disorder: A Dubious Distinction*, a video production, produced by Learning Matters Inc. (588 Broadway, New York, NY 10012) for the Public Broadcasting System, 1995. See www.PBS.org/merrow for information about the full report.

Millar, S. *The Psychology of Play*, 1974, Aronson.

Parry, Sue, conversations with the author on June 4, 2002.

182

BIBLIOGRAPHY

Parry, T., and G. Gregory. *Designing Brain Compatible Learning,* 1998, Skylight Training and Publishing.

Piaget, Jean. *Play, Dreams and Imitation in Childhood,* 1962, Norton.

Schlosberg, H. "The Concept of Play," *Psycol. Rev.,* 54, 229-31, 1947.

Skinner, B. F. *Science and Human Behavior,* 1953, Macmillan.

Sommers, Christina Hoff. *The War Against Boys: How Misguided Feminism Is Harming Our Young Men,* 2000, Simon & Schuster.

Sprenger, M. *Learning and Memory: The Brain in Action,* 1999, Association for Supervision and Curriculum Development.

Tolman, E. C. *Purposive Behavior in Animals and Men,* 1967, University of California Press.

Index

Accountability, 6–8, 61, 65, 150–151. *See also* Parenting, effective; Responsibility

Activities, choosing, 16–18, 159–161

Activity, physical, 41–42

Adoption, books about, 177–178

Advertising, 15–16, 132

Advice, expert, avoiding, 32

Agendas, communicating, 108–109

Alternate reality of children, 96

Arrogance, and control, 30–31, 129–130

Aspirations/goals for children, 26–27, 47

Attention
by children, 29, 43, 96, 103–104, 118–120, 128
by parents, 5, 32, 38, 63–66, 82, 98–99, 104–105, 122–123
by support team members, 63–66
See also Overview role

Babies, innate skills of, 27

Balance, importance of, 159–161

Behavior, of children, 3, 116–121. *See also* Character traits; Child development

Belief systems
cultural and religious, 41
evaluating, 21–23
about parenting, 49–51
positive approach, 132
power of, 111

Blame, accepting. *See* Accountability; Responsibility

Boredom, 35

"Calling," of children, 53–54

Character traits
development process, 121–125
habits, 126–127
versus skills, 128
See also Behavior of children; Child development

Child-centered parenting, 1

Child-centered play, 58

Child development
books about, 175–176
maintaining overview of, 76–77
responding to, 53
supports for, 75–76

184

Child-rearing practices, 3,
47–48. *See also* Parenting,
effective; Upbringing

Child-Rearing Support
System, 86–91

Children
classroom behaviors,
113–114
communications methods,
94–97
defined, 12–13
developmental differences,
56–59
empowering, 101–103
imposing values/agendas
on, 108–109
individuality, uniqueness,
12–13, 18, 22, 63
involving in decision-
making processes, 36,
134, 150, 163–166
learning capacity, 4,
27–28, 53–54
mirroring activities, 21
motivations/preferences,
taking into account,
57–59, 74–75, 94
needs of, 66, 85, 115–116
nonjudgmental nature of,
13
perceptual acumen of,
20–21
power of, 1, 24
preconceptions about, 22
respecting, importance of,
64–65, 72–73, 100, 108,
115–116
scheduling activities for,
79–80

Children (*continued*)
"soul code," 53–54
with special needs, books
about, 170–171
spending time with, 92–93
trusting, 32–33, 58, 100
working with, 60–62,
129–130
See also Attention; Play

Children's fairs, 142–147

Class, social, 49

Classrooms, 112–114

Clinton, Hillary, 33

Coaching skills, 73–74, 98

Communications, by children,
51, 94–97, 99

Communications, effective
books about, 172–173
communicating judg-
ments, 72–73
listening, 94
open communications,
103–104
and realistic expectations,
27
two-way conversations,
98–99

Concentration, as parenting
skill, 60

Connecting to service providers, 141

Consistency, 14, 29–30, 53,
122, 148

Context, for evaluating
programs, 137–138

Control of Nature, The
(McPhee), 129

Control. *See* Managing/
controlling children

Conversations, two-way,
98–99

Cosby, Bill, 62

Courage, as parenting skill, 60

Creativity, toys that foster, 36

Cultural influences, 49

"Culturetocracies," 41, 43

Dedication, as parenting skill,
60

"Default input," 10

Delegating parental authority
benefits/challenges of,
82–84

over-delegation, 92

strategies for, 84–92

Dennis the Menace: The Movie,
88–89

Developmental programs,
75–80. *See also* Child
development; Programs and
support services

Divorce, 3, 102

Dogmatism, 108

Dolls, playing with, 99

Economic realities, 48–49, 87,
93

Empowering children,
102–103

Equal time rule, 112–113

Evaluating programs/services,
80, 141, 165

Expectations
for children, recognizing/
handling, 26–27, 70
for programs/services, 36,
83–85

Extended families, 6–8, 31,
148. *See also* Programs and
support services; Support
system

Fact-gathering, 69

Falling behind in school, 114

Family structure, varieties of,
51, 125

Fatherhood (Cosby), 62

Fearfulness, in children, 60,
91

Fearlessness, of children, 13

Flexibility, as parenting skill,
30, 64, 124

Fragmented lifestyles, 125

Free time, freedom to play,
36–37, 40–41, 58. *See also*
Play; Space and time needs

Friends, as support system,
5–6, 31, 79, 85–86

Fun
as component of
parenting, 107–108
as program goal, 35, 156,
158, 159
See also Free time; Play

Genetics, predispositions,
52–53

Good parenting. *See*
Parenting, effective

Grandparents, 6, 102

Habits, forming, 21, 122, 126–127, 157

Hamasaki, Sachio, 87

Hands-on learning, 36–37

Health, of children, books about, 172–173

Hidden aspects of programs and services, uncovering, 132, 149

Hillman, James, 53

Home, home culture, 54–55, 59

Home enrichment, schooling, books about, 168, 176–177

Humility, 30–31, 129–130

Humor, 63, 72–73, 107, 112, 124

Imagination, 13, 36–37, 39

Impressionability of children, 12, 124

Inconsistency. *See* Consistency

Individuality of children, 63–64, 111–112

Influencing children, 12, 121–122

    approaches to, 24–25

    societal expectations about, 14

    See also Role model, parents as

"Input" actions, 10

Institutions, delegating to, 92, 125. *See also* Support system(s)

Intentions, clarifying, 70

International Association for Child's Right to Play, 58

Internet

    influence of, 2, 90

    research using, 135

Intervening, with service providers, 81

It Takes a Village (Clinton), 33

Judgments, making, 66–67, 80–81

Kagan, Jerome, 92

Knowledge about parenting, lack of, 49–51

Lamphiere, Rebecca, 42

Laughter. *See* Fun; Humor; Play

Learning

    children's capacity for, 4

    individual styles of, 113–114

    interactive, 54

    learning how to learn, 57–59

    self-education, by children, 54

    See also Play

Literacy, basic, 57

Long-term commitments to program/services, 121–122

Long-term effects

    of childhood experiences, 9–10, 40

Long-term effects (*continued*)
of effective parenting, 30, 121–122
of judgment-based messages, 67–69

Love-hate situations, handling, 62

Managing/controlling children, difficulties inherent in, 24–25, 28–29, 40–43, 101, 121, 129

Material resources, and learning, 58

McPhee, John, 129

Medication of children, 3

Mental attitude for selecting/ evaluating services, 148–151

Mentoring, 10–11, 128, 151

Messages
long-term impacts, 67–69
underlying meaning, 120–121

Mimicry, 29–30
children's skill at, 23–24
as learning tool, 40, 42, 53, 58

Mirroring, by children, 21, 121

Modeling. *See* Role model, parents as

Mood, child's, respecting, 72–73

Motivation, child's, working with, 74–75

Nagging, 25, 102

Naïveté, of children, 13

Needs, of children
identifying, 57, 92, 115, 120–121, 160
ignoring, 41, 43, 50–51, 112–113
matching programs to, 149–150, 157–160
respecting, 37, 39, 55, 64, 115–116

Negative influences, 2, 31, 43, 151–153

Negotiating for services, 146–147

Nicknames, 113

"No choice" option, 10, 16

Nonjudgmental behavior, 13, 66–67, 97

Nonverbal communications, 94–95. *See also* Communications

Nurturing environment, importance of, 55, 58

Observation
prior to action, 65, 97
seeing beneath the surface, 35, 151–153

Open-ended questions
asking during evaluation, 149
as communication tool, 116–117

"Othering," 54, 87–88

Over delegating, 92–93

Overview of programs/ services, 17, 90, 137–141

OVERVIEW – PLAY

Overview role, 13, 18, 76–77, 82, 139–140

Overworked America (Schor), 22–23

Parental authority
and control, 101
delegating, 2, 5, 31–36, 75–94

Parenting, effective
accepting blame, 14, 150–151
active involvement, 55, 64–66, 92–93
books about, 169–170
characteristics of, 29–31, 59–61, 103–109
coaching skills, 73–74
delegating authority, 2, 5, 31–36, 75–94
empowering children, 102–103
flexibility, 64
handling expectations, 26–27
judgment-making process, 65–73
listening, 94
management style, 28–29
mentoring, coaching role, 10–11, 164
nurturing attitude, 55
overview role, 16–18, 76–77, 104, 137–138
playfulness, 41, 105–108
recognizing individuality, 63–64

Parenting, effective (*continued*)
tweaking, 130
working with children, 61–62

Parenting skills, need to learn, 5–7, 47

"Parentocracies," 41, 43

Parents, parenting
factors that affect, 3, 48–54
importance of, 7–8, 13
incompetent, 150–151
power of, over children, 5–6
as role model, 21

Participating in child's life, 55, 64–66, 92–93

People CARE (People Concerned About Recess in Education), 42

Perfectionism, 83

Performance, in school, 115

Permissiveness, 7

Personality, of children, 63–64

Perspective. *See* Overview role

Physical contact, 96, 101

Physical presence, importance of, 65–66. *See also* Attention

Piaget, Jean, 39–40

Planning process, for program/service selection, 134

Play
by adults, 23
books about, 169
child-centered, 58
choosing programs that encourage, 99

Play (*continued*)

communicating using, 96–99

defined, 39

importance of, 1, 34, 39–43

and learning, 58–59

See also Space and time needs

Politeness. *See* Respect

Pontification, 108

Positive approach, 105–106

Preconceptions, 21–24

Privilege, parenting as, 1

Privacy, child's, respecting, 96, 100

Proactive behaviors, 131

Problem behaviors

creative solutions, 119–120

evaluating honestly, 116–119

Products for children, evaluating, 16–18, 34–36

Programs, support services

achieving balance, 159–161

expectations, realistic, 36

choosing wisely, 16–18, 75–76

evaluating, 34–35, 80–81, 131–134, 142–151, 166

having backup plans, 164–165

intervening if appropriate, 81

invisible aspects of, 151–153

Programs (*continued*)

involving children in selecting, 134, 163–166

maintaining overview of, 76–77

negotiating for, 146–147

observing, 80

researching, strategies for, 131–141

scheduling, 79–80

selection process, 77–79, 140–141, 156–159, 163–164

working with, 81–82

Questions

of children, taking seriously, 97

importance of asking, 133

open-ended, 98

Recess, efforts to eliminate, 41–42

Religious beliefs/religious organizations

focus on work, 41, 43

and parenting style, 49, 125

programs incorporating, 157

Researching programs. *See* Programs and support services

Respecting children, 64–65, 72–73, 100, 108, 115–116

Responsibility, parental versus control, 41

Responsibility (*continued*)

delegating, 11, 79, 87, 90, 128

importance of, 14, 66, 128, 150–151

as legal responsibility, 77

for managing programs/ services, 79

for nurturing, 55

See also Parenting, effective

Role model, parents as, 21, 121, 125

Roosevelt, Eleanor, 13

Scheduling activities, 15, 34, 37, 79–80, 152

Schools, school systems

"equal" treatment of children, 112–113

helping children handle, 115–116

selecting, 78–79

work versus play at, 43

Schor, Juliet, 22–23

Seeking skills, 131–134

Selecting programs and services, 141, 148–151, 156–159

Self-education, by children, 54

Selling of programs/services, 142–143, 145

Services for children. *See* Programs, support services

Shyness

identifying root causes, 116–117

Shyness (*continued*)

response to, in classrooms, 113

as survival strategy, 118–119

Single-parent families, 3, 174–175

Skill mentoring, 128

Skills, of children, 39, 127–128

Skills, parenting, 7–8, 30, 42, 49–50, 148. *See also* Parenting, effective

"Soul's code" (Hillman), 53

Space and time needs, 34, 40, 55, 58, 101

Stability, of home base, 55

Standing watch. *See* Overview role

Stimulation, need for, 56

Structured time, 36. *See also* Space and time needs

Styles of parenting, 107–108

Subnuclear families, 2, 93, 125

Substitutes for parents, 2, 5–6, 15–16. *See also* Programs, support services; Support system(s)

Success, different views of, 115–116

Supervision, 7, 35, 61

Support system(s)

friends, 5–6, 31, 79, 85–86

importance of, 31–32, 60, 75–76, 125

"othering" relationships, 86–88, 122

Support system(s) (*continued*)
seeking out, 128, 131–141
team approach, 81–82
See also Programs, support
services

Supportive behaviors, 102–103

Szasz, Thomas, 165

Talent, of others, making use
of, 85–86

"Teachertocracies," 41, 43

Teachers, 112–113, 115

Teamwork
with children, 98
with service providers,
81–82

Telephone tree, 88–89

Time spent parenting
divorced parents, 102
factors that attenuate, 48
and influence, 52, 92–93,
122
length of process, 47–48

Timing, of communications,
70–71

Toys, 36, 168

Training
of children, 71, 97, 124,
128
for parents, 7–8, 30, 42,
49–50, 148
of support team members,
90

Trial periods, 157

Trust
in children, importance of,
32–33, 58
earning, 1, 60–61, 70
helping children develop,
60–61, 100
in self, 31
in support team members,
11, 78, 81, 90–91

Tweaking, 130

Unconditional love/support,
60, 66, 76

Unintentional actions, 10

Upbringing, 3
books about, 176
creating nurturing envi-
ronment, 14, 18, 59–60
defined, 9-10
mentoring component,
10–11

Values, of parents, 5, 108–109

Verbal communications,
95–96

Vision, helping children
achieve, 107

Work versus play, 41. *See also*
Play

Working with children,
60–62, 129–130

Writing down ideas, 85, 159

DIRECT ORDER FORM

Email orders: unwindology@hawaii.rr.com. Please send information requested on this form.

Phone orders: Toll-free (888) 969-6872

Fax orders: (808) 988-9507. Please send this form.

Postal orders: Unwindology Publishing, P.O. Box 61009, Honolulu, HI 96822. USA. Telephone: (808) 255-4710.

Please send ____ *copies of the book, The Privilege of Parenting.*
I understand that I may return them for a full refund for any reason, no questions asked.

Name _____

Address _____

City _____

State _____ Zip _____ - _____

Telephone _____

email address _____

Excise tax: Please add 4.13% for products shipped to Hawaii addresses.

Shipping by air:

US: $4 for the first book and $2 for each additional book.

International: $9 for first book and $5 for each additional book (estimate).

Payment: ❏ Check ❏ Visa ❏ MasterCard ❏ Discover

Card number _____

Name on card _____ Exp. _____

Authorization signature _____

Website:
www.unwindology.com
Where people go to regain perspective